The

John Harris was educated at Rotherham Grammar School and first worked as a reporter on the *Sheffield Telegraph*. He later joined the Merchant Navy but at the outbreak of the Second World War enlisted in the RAF, serving in Africa and from 1941-45 in air/sea rescue launches. He wrote many bestselling books.

Also by John Harris

Dunkirk

JOHN HARRIS

THE
SOMME

CANELOHISTORY

First published in the United Kingdom in 1966 by Hodder & Stoughton

This edition published in the United Kingdom in 2022 by

Canelo
Unit 9, 5th Floor
Cargo Works, 1–2 Hatfields
London, SE1 9PG
United Kingdom

A CIP catalogue record for this book is available from the British Library.

Print ISBN 978 1 80032 855 6
Ebook ISBN 978 1 80032 563 0

Look for more great books at www.canelo.co

Printed and bound in Great Britain by Clays Ltd, Elcograf S.p.A.

Author's note

The Somme was not one single battle, but a series of battles lasting from July 1st to November 18th, 1916, and each of these was made up of minor engagements, some of which had no name beyond that of the trench involved. To attempt to describe the whole period in detail would be confusing to the reader. Instead, I have tried to give a broad picture, concentrating on the sound and the feel and the smell – which, after all, is as much the stuff of history as dates and figures.

One: The big show

7-30 a.m. July 1st, 1916

The First World War – the greatest war the world had ever seen, in which millions were to die and millions more were to suffer mutilation – began for England on August 4th, 1914, and for nearly two years the British Army, with its French allies, had faced the Germans across a strip of stale, stagnant No Man's Land in France and Belgium.

This slender ribbon of churned-up ground, criss-crossed by rusty barbed wire and littered with all the ugly rubbish of war, lay between two sets of opposing trenches, which ran all the way from the North Sea to the Vosges, a miry series of fortifications that represented the dead hopes of military and political leaders on both sides. The opposing armies had fought constantly across this same narrow area of bloodstained ground. Occasionally, a salient – which was the high-sounding name given by military men to a dent in the line – would be bitten off, or another, which was the futile finishing point of some ambitious attack costing thousands of lives, would be thrust out. But, on the whole, the position of the line had hardly changed since October 1914, when the open warfare of the first months of the fighting had ended and siege operations had begun.

While in Russia the armies had marched and counter-marched, with elbow-room to manoeuvre against each other for a killing position, in the West they had remained static. Attempts by either side to advance had resulted only in slaughter; and the troops, watching the daily drainage of men in trench warfare, had grown cynical and desperate at the obvious inability of the staff to find a way through the enemy's lines.

But now, in mid-1916, the vast mass of Kitchener's New Armies had arrived in France and a new spirit had appeared. The defeats of the previous year had been blamed on the scandalous shortage of shells and this had now been overcome by the electric personality of David Lloyd George, the fiery little Welshman from Criccieth, whose criticism had turned the government upside-down. A great new effort was about to be made to smash the German line for good and all, to put an end to trench warfare. The biggest assault yet mounted in this or any previous war was ready to be launched.

Along the whole British front in Picardy, from Hannescamps north of the River Ancre to Maricourt near the River Somme – a distance of twenty-five miles – men of the British Army crouched in their trenches to begin their advance against the German positions on the slopes opposite. There were 100,000 of them ready to go over the top in the first tremendous waves and there were another 400,000 in support. Behind them, guns were massed in their hundreds, one to every yard of front, and along the lines of communication there were thousands of carts, lorries, tractors and trains to bring up supplies and reserves. South of Maricourt – on both sides of the River Somme – the same preparations had been made in the French sector.

Gathered between the Somme and the Ancre was virtually the entire strength of the British Expeditionary Force. A few of the new civilian-soldiers had fought at Gallipoli or at Loos, but for most this was their first real trial of strength. Almost every British fighting soldier on the field was a New Army man – for even in the old regular battalions, decimated at Mons, Ypres and Loos, fresh strength had been drawn from the same sources as the brand-new battalions. It was a brand-new army, in fact, with brand-new equipment and a brand-new spirit, the biggest and undoubtedly the finest in brains, physique and education that Britain had ever put into the field.

There were units from Bermuda and Newfoundland, and Colonials who had sold all they possessed to pay their own fare home from the farthest corners of the earth – Boers who had fought against England not so very long before, and soldiers of fortune who had seen service with the Japanese, the Egyptians and even with Pancho Villa's rebels in Mexico. Many of them were mere boys, some even under age, others men of sixty who had joined up to avenge the deaths of sons lost in the first staggering battles of 1914 and 1915. There were veterans of the Zulu and the Ashanti campaigns of the previous century, old men who couldn't resist a scrap, men who had been brought up in the period of England's imperialistic conquests and felt they must have just one more go.

Every single man was a volunteer, for although conscription had at last been introduced, it had not yet begun to send trained fighting men to the front.

Some of those in uniform might well have served their country better at their lathes and benches – indeed, many had been unwillingly combed out and sent home to train others in the vast expansion of the munitions industry. And a tremendous number of the men in the ranks were potential officers – university graduates, steel experts, chemists, lawyers, business heads, the sort of men who, in the Second World War, rapidly moved on to more responsible tasks after their initial training. Often these men had competed for places in their battalions like candidates in a short list for a new job; with their intelligence, initiative and capacity for leadership, they were going to be sadly missed before the war was over.

Battery on battery on battery of guns, light and heavy, were placed wheel to wheel, sending up whorls of white Picardy chalk-dust and setting the transport animals shying as they fired. For once, the men had been told, there was no shortage of shells. Lloyd George had seen to that.

They knew, as they looked up at the German-occupied slopes ahead of them, that there were likely to be casualties, but the thoughts of fear were overlaid by the exhilaration and the importance of the occasion.

Lord Kitchener, the god-like figure who had made their corporate whole possible, was dead – drowned when the cruiser taking him to Russia had struck a mine – and he, like the victims of the Zeppelin raids on England, had to be avenged. Although Asquith's discredited government of muddle and 'wait and see' was still in being, it was tottering to its end, and Lloyd George was secure at the War Office so all was well.

The Battle of Jutland had put paid to the German Fleet; Verdun, the great conflict to the south, which had drawn away so many Frenchmen from the Somme, was quietening down; and the Russian offensive was in full swing. Now it was their turn – England's turn. This battle, they believed, was going to affect the whole future of the world – as indeed it did, though scarcely in the way they thought.

July 1st had dawned a perfect day for the attack. There was a brilliant blue sky and mist in the hollows near the river. The orders of Sir Douglas Haig, the Commander-in-Chief, had made it clear that this was to be the great break-through that would carry them into open country again, beyond the trenches and barbed wire and dug-outs and the old unburied dead, so that at last the cavalry massed behind could hurry through and turn north to take the enemy defences in rear.

Everyone had known about the attack for weeks, months even. In England, which to those going on leave already seemed 'queer and foreign', more seemed to be known by the civilians than by the soldiers at the front. The attack was talked of there as "The Big Push" and "The Big Show". It was to be a cake-walk. All they had to do, they had been confidently told by their commanders, once the vast barrage had shattered every defensive position before them, was to walk over and take possession of the ruins.

There was a momentary silence as the bombarding artillery shifted its ranges and the falling shells moved on to the second objectives, then the whistles went and the men struggled up the ladders and through the newly dug debouching exits that led to the gaps in their wire and into No Man's Land, and began their slow trudge towards the German lines.

By nightfall, almost 60,000 of them were dead or wounded, and the survivors, shocked and dazed, were back in their own trenches, for the most part having achieved nothing.

They were only the first. In the next four and a half months half a million more were to follow them to hospitals or to the muddy graveyards among the scattered copses and knuckled hills of the Somme.

Two: Breaking strains

The war had started almost by accident. Nobody had wanted it and nobody had expected it, though unbearable tensions had been building up for years.

Germany, originally a number of unimportant states that had torn each other apart in the religious struggles of the Thirty Years' War, had been growing in power since Waterloo. By the middle of the nineteenth century, the German princelings had been drawing together under the house of Hohenzollern, and the dominant force in this embryo nation had been the Prussians, the most vital and dynamic of the Germanic peoples. Bismarck, chief architect of the new unified Germany, had been able in 1864, with Austria's help, to defeat Denmark and, two years later, turning on his old ally, he had ended Austrian predominance among the German nations, and was able to form the northern states into the North German Confederation under Prussia's leadership. In 1870, he manoeuvred Prussia's old enemy, France, into a position where she rushed into a disastrous war that lost her Alsace and Lorraine.

His final triumph was to have the Prussian King William I crowned German Emperor at Versailles.

The French, remembering their greatness under Louis XIV and later under Napoleon I, reacted bitterly to the defeat of 1870. All their subsequent political and military thinking was dominated by ideas of revenge. Laying the blame on the fumbling tactics of Napoleon III and his court generals, they began to think in terms of attack, attack, attack, with Germany always the enemy.

But, by 1914, in addition to the growing nationalism of Germany and the humiliated anti-German hatred of France, other stresses and strains were at work in Europe – chief among them the desire of Russia for an interest in the Slav Balkans where Austria was the dominant force, and the mounting anxiety of Britain at the increasing aggressiveness of Germany.

After Waterloo, Britain had emerged as the most powerful and respected of the European nations, but the industrial expansion that followed, with its insistence on commerce and wealth, had blunted her vision. Under the stifling reign of Victoria, the vital spirit of the nation had all too often been submerged in the rigid national respect for elders and betters personified in the ageing queen, and in jingoistic imperialism. England had begun to feel she was the greatest nation in the world and could afford to sit back and rest on her laurels.

The sudden upsurge of confidence in Germany – which sprang from her alarming industrial, commercial and military strength – brought Britain up with a jolt and she began to look anxiously at the new alignments in Europe.

–

After the war of 1870, Germany and France, each in an endeavour to strengthen herself against the other, had formed alliances – Germany with Austria and Italy, and France with Russia. Though Britain had held aloof from these continental pacts, she had been drawn on the whole not towards France, a traditional enemy, but towards what she considered her German "cousins".

German jealousy of Britain, however, had been growing since the turn of the century. The German Emperor, William II, hinted that only the superiority of the British Navy had prevented him from joining in the Boer War on the opposing side; and, obsessed by his envy for British naval power, he began to build up his own fleet.

At last, British statesmen realised that it would be suicidal to remain on bad terms with France. Under the premiership of Balfour, an Entente Cordiale was negotiated, which included a "gentleman's agreement" that each would support the other in case of an attack. A few years later a similar understanding was reached between Britain and France's ally, Russia.

Meanwhile Admiral Sir John Fisher had designed a new superbattleship, the Dreadnought, which would outrange and out-steam anything afloat, while Lord Haldane at the War Office reorganised Britain's old colonial army to fit it for a possible war against a European power.

Then, unexpectedly, on June 28th, 1914, just when the tension between the powers seemed to be relaxing a little, the Hapsburg Archduke Franz Ferdinand, heir to the throne of Austria, and his wife were assassinated in Sarajevo by young Slav patriots who wished the Austrian provinces of Bosnia and Herzegovina to be joined to their natural mother country, Serbia, instead of to the Hapsburgs.

The event, in itself, seemed unimportant. In fact, most people in England were inclined to regard assassination as one of the occupational hazards of central European princes. But it was in fact the event that started the greatest war the world had known, which was to engulf monarchies and start the overthrow of the old order of things everywhere in the world.

Austria decided to make an example of Serbia and sent her an ultimatum. On July 25th, Serbia accepted the terms, but with reservations, and Austria, determined to carry the humiliation to the limit, broke off diplomatic relations. As it happened, she was only bluffing but the act proved to be the spark that lit the general conflagration.

In the tense years before, the powerful European countries had built up vast conscript armies, and now all the alliances and agreements that had been made earlier came into force. Mobilisation began and war came nearer, like a juggernaut that, once set in motion, cannot be stopped. Statesmen miscalculated, and threats that had worked on other occasions this time proved ineffective. And the great armies that had been built to provide security against aggression carried the nations into battle by their own tremendous weight. Russia, the protector of the Balkan Slavs, was drawn in, then Germany and France; and finally when the Germans – in an attempt to outflank the French fortifications – marched into Belgium, England. The war that nobody had wanted had started.

–

Chiefs-of-staff on both sides had planned for an aggressive war, and France, in her anxiety not to repeat the hesitancy that had lost her the war of 1870, advanced at once into a bold campaign in Lorraine. She had, however, underrated German strength and the flower of her armies was destroyed with ease. Meanwhile, the Germans, following a plan made by Count von Schlieffen during his period of office as Chief of the German Staff from 1892 to 1906, had swept round in a great arc through Belgium and, finding practically nothing in their path, had plunged forward almost to Paris. The French, who had gone to war still in the uniforms of the Second Empire – blue coats and red trousers, their officers even wearing white gloves – and with their troops riding on cannon decorated with flowers, had fallen back in retreat; and the small but highly efficient British Expeditionary Force had been dragged into battle almost before it was ready.

Belgium and Northern France had become full of retreating refugees, their household goods packed into landaus, farmcarts, even prams; and heat-exhausted soldiers, their backs chafed by the rub of unfamiliar entrenching spades, had stumbled westwards behind army wagons pulled by worn horses still restless in their brand-new harness.

The war of movement had lasted only a matter of weeks, however, and then the newly developed and deadly machine gun and the high explosive shell had forced the system of trench warfare on all the armies involved. Trenches had gradually extended outwards from the initial meeting point, as the belligerents sought a way round each other's flanks, until they reached the North Sea at one end and the mountains to the north of Switzerland at the other. All the great battles of 1915 had been fought by the Allies with the vain hope of smashing a hole through the German fortifications so that the war of movement could begin once again.

But the advantage was always with Germany. She was sitting in the centre of a circle of fortifications, with her enemies around her on the outside:

it was always easier for her to rush reserves to any trouble spot than it was for the Allies. The result was that, again and again, attacks in the east and west petered out with the same disastrous results. At long last, the four allied powers, France, Russia, Britain and Italy (Italy had broken her agreement with Germany and come in on the side of the Allies) realised that the prime need was to attack simultaneously with their maximum forces on their respective fronts, in order to overcome the Austro-German advantage of interior lines of communication.

The Battle of the Somme was the natural outcome of this discovery.

Three: "Your country needs you"

The Somme was not only a ferocious contest between two great powers; it was also the climax of an emotion – an emotion that reached its fullness just before July 1st, 1916. After the battle, it withered and was never the same again.

This emotion was symbolised in the character of Field-Marshal Lord Kitchener, England's most respected soldier, the conqueror of the Sudan and the man who had brought the Boer War to an end. He had been Commander-in-Chief, India, and in 1914 was virtual ruler of Egypt but, by chance, he happened to be in England when war broke out and, in a desire to give some weight to the shaky prestige of the Liberal War Cabinet, the Prime Minister, Asquith, had appointed him War Minister.

A military autocrat who found it almost impossible to get along with politicians, Kitchener had a brilliant if somewhat undeserved reputation. Instead of the master organiser he was believed to be, he was in fact, in the words of one of his warmest admirers, a smasher of organisations, a master of expedients. Though he had led armies, he had never led a battalion in action and his mind was devoid of the imagination that makes a great commander. Yet, for all his faults, he had from time to time flashes of intuition, which aided him greatly in his career. And in 1914, when everyone else was predicting that the war would be "over by Christmas", he foresaw that England was about to face the greatest trial in her history. He announced that the war would last for three or four years and that an army of many millions would be needed.

Unlike the Continental powers, however, Britain had no system of conscription to give her such troops and had to rely instead on volunteers. Machinery for providing them already existed in the Territorial Army, but Kitchener despised these "Town Clerk's soldiers", as he called them, and set out to raise independently a new regular force of 70 divisions – Kitchener's Army or the New Army, as it began to be called. His picture glared balefully down from every hoarding in the country, forefinger outstretched, intimidating and accusing, "Your Country Needs You".

Kitchener had counted on getting 100,000 volunteers in the first six months and maybe

500,000 altogether – as much as the existing factories could hope to equip – but his plans were submerged in a wave of patriotic enthusiasm. 500,000 volunteered in the first month, and thereafter recruits came in at a rate of over 100,000 a month. Altogether, Britain raised more than 3,000,000 volunteers before conscription was introduced early in 1916, and neither Kitchener nor the government knew what to do with them.

Yet recruitment had been slow to start. Young men from shops and offices and from good positions in industry and commerce had seen the posters and heard such songs as *We Don't Want To Lose You But We Think You Ought To Go*, but had never thought the appeals were addressed to them. They hadn't private incomes, so they felt themselves excluded from holding commissions, and they knew they weren't the class from which the rank and file of the army was normally recruited. So in the first days of the war, they carried on as usual and wondered where Kitchener would get all the recruits he was demanding.

But then had come the startling and unexpected news of disaster from Mons, where the British Expeditionary Force had blundered into the

German masses on August 22nd and been forced back in a precipitous retreat, and they suddenly realised that Kitchener meant them. There was a rush to join up. On August 8th, 1914, Kitchener asked for his first 100,000; within three weeks he had them in camp.

Many volunteers passed a whole day in the broiling August sunshine, waiting to enlist, sometimes even sleeping the night in ditches or on the pavement, while extra policemen had to be brought in to control the crowds. Since Kitchener refused to use the Territorial organisation, the Regular Army machinery was called upon to deal with unprecedented numbers and creaked rather badly. But the first white-hot enthusiasm overcame all difficulties, and young men were swept along by the excitement of those golden afternoons.

The new armies, often wearing the old-fashioned blue because khaki was short, and often without uniforms at all, trained in parks and squares, using broomsticks to practice bayonet fighting, their few items of equipment hung about their persons with pieces of string. Among them were young poets such as Siegfried Sassoon, "with a feeling of being dedicated to death and not in the least perturbed by the idea," and Rupert Brooke, who spoke for an entire generation: "Now God be thanked Who has matched us with His hour."

With the great gun of the Grand Fleet between them and the danger of invasion, these young Britishers had a different attitude to the war from their French counterparts. Unlike their allies, they were going into battle for a cause – to protect the neutrality and independence of Belgium – and they talked from the beginning in idealistic terms. For them, it was not a war of conquest or defence, but "the war to end war" and "to make the world safe for democracy".

Their high spirits swept them into the ranks of the new battalions. To the alert intelligent ones, the faults of the old army were glaringly obvious, but because of their idealism, they didn't complain, enduring the hardships of unfinished camps, appalling food and indifferent leadership with great good humour. They continued to work at becoming soldiers even when the day's training programme had come to an end; and crime was almost unknown, a fact that puzzled N.C.O.s of the old army, who were used to the ragtag and bobtail of the nation.

Young men of good families were offered commissions, and so were regular N.C.O.s and men who had proved their worth. In addition, Kitchener recalled to the colours retired N.C.O.s to become the backbone of the new armies. Brigadier-General F. P. Crozier, at that time a young officer helping with the formation of an Ulster battalion, met a detachment of them in London and found among them men of up to sixty-five and beyond, dyeing their hair and keeping out of sight the medals that gave away their age.

The newcomers were fed atrocity stories to rouse their blood-lust – though many were too intelligent to believe them – and even the Church was called upon to make the war appear a crusade. Playgrounds and open spaces all over England began to fill up with men and horses and wagons as equipment began to arrive, and by the spring of 1915 the new recruits had become soldiers with a sturdy independence, modelled neither on the Territorials nor on the Regulars. Everywhere they marched they were greeted by hordes of children and flags. Their spirit was magnificent: their chief fear was that the war would be over before they had had a chance to take part in it.

The tragedy was that, although a few of their commanders were men on leave from France or officers of the Indian Army who chanced to be in England, too often they were "dug-outs" – elderly retired men who had long since put aside their regimentals; and the junior officers, though keen as mustard, were entirely lacking in experience.

The subalterns were taught to conduct themselves in battle in the only manner known to their trainers, who had learned their lessons in colonial wars leading the riff-raff who had made up the old army: they must expose themselves recklessly under fire to give their men courage, a behaviour highly dangerous against machine guns and modern rifles in the hands of trained men. And in most cases, they were unable to rely on their N.C.O.s to put right their mistakes, because some of these N.C.O.s were giving orders of forty years before while others were just as inexperienced as their officers and had been dragged from the ranks merely because of a loud voice or a fine figure.

Nevertheless, their enthusiasm was tremendous – in spite of occasional disturbing encounters with men in bright blue hospital suits who held crutches against stiff legs or drank left-handed because they had no right hands. These men, often bitterly cynical, told them stories of blundering that chilled their blood; and from tired-eyed officers, newly commissioned from the ranks, they began to hear that real fighting was not quite the same as the theoretical stuff they'd been learning. They discovered, to their surprise, that the pick and the shovel were almost as important as the rifle; that it was more useful to be able to shoot fast than accurately; and that bombs and bludgeons had far more part in trench fighting than ceremonial swords and bayonets.

It was puzzling and a little worrying at times, but they were not dismayed. When eventually their units were sent to the front, all efforts by the authorities to keep their departure secret were defeated by the parades and the bands, and by the arms and heads sprouting from troop trains as they moved to the ports. They were off at last to win the war.

Four: The plan

"A sense of the inevitable broods over the battle-fields of the Somme," said Winston Churchill who all along opposed the offensive. "The British armies were so ardent, their leaders so confident, the need and appeals of our allies so clamant, and decisive results seemingly so near that no human power could have prevented the attempt."

The idea of the battle was first put forward on December 6th, 1915, at a military conference at Chantilly, where the Allied leaders in the east and west agreed to make their offensive simultaneously. The men who made the decision and who were to direct the battle were the cream of the pre-war army, men who had started their service under Victoria and were products of a military age far removed from the Western Front of 1916. The troops they commanded were as different as chalk from cheese from the forces they were used to leading, and the enemy were not those they knew from colonial wars. But their minds, unimaginative and narrow, could conceive no other form of attack than the frontal assaults to which they had grown accustomed.

Some men, however, had looked at larger maps than those of the immediate "front", and had suggested assaults, not on the field of the enemy's choice, but on the comparatively unprotected part of the German Empire – through the back door, so to speak. These men, led by Winston Churchill, had reluctantly been given their chance to prove their theory at Gallipoli in 1915. But the brass-hats of the Army, Kitchener among them, had never felt able to commit themselves sufficiently to the idea to send enough troops or supplies, and the strategy had failed. The supporters of the wider sphere of war never recovered from the disaster at Gallipoli, and from then on, the frontal attack in France, which had already proved so costly, was the only method of warfare that was considered by the High Command.

Casualties, unfortunately, had proved heavier than had seemed possible. In January 1916, conscription for bachelors was introduced and Lloyd George, a man with a reputation for getting things done, was made Minister of Munitions to put right the shortages on which were blamed the defeat at Neuve Chapelle in 1915. This was a mismanaged attempt to break the German line that had ended as usual in failure.

The year 1915 reached its close with the advantage still with Germany, as it was to remain throughout the four years of hostilities. The Germans had already conquered Belgium and the whole of Northern France, and they had only to hang on to their gains to win the war. The onus was on the Allies to drive them back over the frontier. No matter how many Germans were killed, the Allies could never claim victory while a single German soldier remained on French or Belgian soil, and it was this urgent necessity that shaped all the allied plans. The Germans had to be driven back, and 1916 was selected as the year of the great effort that was – and had to be – made.

The moving spirit behind the decision was General Joffre, the French Chief-of-Staff. It was Joseph Jacques Cesaire Joffre who had been responsible for the disastrous Plan XVII of 1914, which had destroyed the French armies in Lorraine, though – not entirely deservedly – he had recouped some of his lost reputation by refusing to panic at the chaos that resulted.

Sixty-two years of age, he was an engineer who had become Chief of the French General Staff in 1911. He had fought in the war of 1870 and seen service in several colonial campaigns, but his comparatively slight experience was not supplemented by any very adequate training in the theory of war, and when he reached the Higher Command he had to apply himself to the study of an art that his contemporaries had been teaching for years. In compensation for his many faults, however, he had one great gift – the ability to remain unflustered in the midst of disaster, and his very impassivity had been a steadying influence in the early days of 1914. Moreover, he was one of the few men farsighted enough to expect a long war.

To Joffre, whose armies had borne the burden of fighting the Germans alone for almost two years while the British were building up their army, the decision to make an attack in the west seemed simple and straightforward. Yet when he came to formulate the plan, solid squarely-built "Papa" Joffre found himself at loggerheads with the newly appointed Commander-in-Chief of the British Expeditionary Force, Sir Douglas Haig.

Haig, a dour Scot, was more suited by temperament to defence than to attack. Like many of the other British leaders who had come to the top after the Boer War, he was a cavalryman. Fifty-four years of age and typical of his class, he was wealthy, educated at public school and Oxford, a prize-winner at Sandhurst, and a graduate of the Staff College, where, however, he seems to have been thoroughly unpopular with his contemporaries. He had been a staff officer with Kitchener at Khartoum, and with Sir John French in South Africa, but his acquaintance with battle before 1914 had been as fleeting as Joffre's. Like Joffre again, he had a cool head but, unlike Joffre, he was agonisingly shy with strangers. Nevertheless, he had many influential friends, chief among them King George V.

He had not been above intriguing for the removal of his predecessor, Sir John French, at the end of 1915, but in outlining French's errors he had tended to overlook his own shortcomings and his diary contains no sign of self-reproach or admission of mistakes. He had always distrusted the French with an insularity that was typical of his day and age, but he was fearless and handsome, a perfect example, it seemed, of a good general

– immaculate well-connected, studious in military matters, sober, religious and patriotic. It was not so well known, however, that he was intolerant of other people's opinions, lacking in magnetism and unable to understand the ordinary man in the trenches, whom he rarely managed to see or meet. And one of his chief faults was his habit of picking for his staff men who told him what he wanted to hear, yes-men who were unable to disagree with him when disagreement was important.

For all the old-world charm he could turn on at will, he was an ambitious, vain man, obsessed with a belief in cavalry. And though he had managed to win, quite undeservedly, the confidence of the British fighting soldier, thousands of these soldiers were to die because he had not learned the power of modern weapons in defence or the futility of frontal attacks on heavily entrenched positions. He has been described as "so unimaginative that he could not see that the tactics of the past were as dead as mutton" and one of his contemporaries said of him: "If I was opposed by Haig, I should always know what he would do."

–

When the decision to launch a concentrated attack against the Germans was made, it seemed to Haig as he studied his maps that the best place for the assault in the west would be in Flanders, particularly if it could coincide with a naval landing on the coast. Joffre had other ideas and insisted on the Somme.

It seemed a strange choice for a battlefield, since, as there had been practically no fighting there for two years, the Germans had been able to construct for themselves one of the strongest defensive positions of their whole line. John Masefield, who later became the Poet Laureate, after he had visited the front said: "Almost in every part our men had to go uphill to attack... The enemy had look-out posts with fine views... Our men were down below with no view of anything but stronghold after stronghold just up above being made stronger daily."

Because of the bare nature of the territory and the absence of railways, there could never be any immediate objectives on the Somme, but the wily Joffre had had two good reasons for his choice of ground. He was well aware that the German position was a strong one, which the enemy would be loath to abandon, and would fight hard to retain: the inevitable result would be a battle of attrition

– the *bataille d'usure*, which he liked so well. He also shared the feeling, common among French officers, that the British had not been pulling their weight hitherto. Here, at the junction of the two armies, they would be obliged to become "involved".

These subtle motives escaped not only his allies but also the Germans, who were never able to understand the preparations that began to be made on the Somme. Von Falkenhayn, the German Chief-of-Staff, in fact, could never bring himself to believe – even when the offensive was imminent – that the German Second Army could possibly be attacked on that front.

The decision was made, however, and it was to bring death or mutilation to a generation and an end to the idealism with which thousands of young men had rushed to join the army.

The plan produced at Chantilly followed almost exactly the wishes of "Papa" Joffre. It was decided that the Western Front was to be the primary theatre of war and that there should be an enormous assault on a front of sixty miles across the River Somme. The place was suggested in a note to Haig as early as December 30th, 1915. "The ground," said Joffre, "is in many places favourable to the development of a powerful offensive," and brushing aside Haig's preference for Flanders, he claimed that the rolling uplands of Picardy were far more suitable than the marshy lands to the north. If the attack could really be got moving, he said, the elbow room that would be available would enable the allied armies to swing north or south according to which way the battle went.

Haig, whose preference for Flanders was to be proved as wrong the following year at Passchendaele as Joffre's choice of Picardy was proved wrong in 1916, eventually agreed. He almost invariably gave way to French wishes, though he had been firmly told by Kitchener that his command was an independent one and that "in no case was he to come under the orders of any allied general".

Joffre now began to develop the idea of a series of preliminary attacks to wear down the Germans before the main assault. Haig, the meticulous trainer of troops, preferred, however, to conserve his armies for one great effort. At this stage it was understood that the French would take the major share of the assault with 39 French divisions against the 25 to 30 British divisions.

By February 11th, the main details had been decided, except for the date. The assault was clearly impossible for the spring, because neither the British, nor the Russians, who were to mount a simultaneous attack in the east, could be ready by then, but the month of July was mentioned as the most likely time.

Long before that, however, an event occurred that changed the whole set-up and made what was to have been largely a French battle into an almost exclusively British one, an event that neither Joffre nor Haig had ever allowed for.

The Germans at Verdun started their battle of attrition first.

–

Lieutenant-General Erich von Falkenhayn, the Chief of the German General Staff, had never thought that victory could be achieved on the Eastern Front; he guessed that success there would only draw the Germans, like Napoleon's Grand Army in 1812 and Hitler's armies in the War of 1939, deeper and deeper into hostile territory without destroying the Russians. Great Britain, in his view, was the arch-enemy and must be deprived of her continental ally, France, before the war could be won.

He knew of the enormous losses of France in 1914 and of her dwindling reserves, and his idea was to bleed her white so that she would have to withdraw from the combat. Then the British would be driven to make peace, leaving the Germans still occupying the lands they had conquered. His plan was almost an exact counterpart of Joffre's. It was not strategy. It was the same simple policy of attrition. And Falkenhayn had found the obvious fortress for which the French would fight, in just the same way that Joffre expected the Germans to fight for the Somme – Verdun, at the head of an awkward salient in the French line, a city that the French people, quite wrongly, believed to be the cornerstone of their defences.

Joffre was warned of the approaching attack but, obsessed with his plans for the Somme, did nothing to repair the neglected defences of the city. On February 21st, 1916, the battle of Verdun started when a 14-inch German shell exploded in the palace of the Archbishop.

Five: Verdun

Verdun produced the first of the tremendous bombardments that were to characterise the fighting of 1916. The French line, sagging under the weight of the high explosive that was hurled at it, began to give east of the Meuse. Joffre sent little help, however, and would not allow the new threat to interfere with his plans for his own attack later in the year.

Aristide Briand, the French Prime Minister, took a different view. It was useless for Joffre's staff to point out that Verdun, badly supplied and with difficult lines of communication, was in fact an embarrassment and really of no importance. Whatever the staff might think, he argued, the rest of France would certainly consider its loss a defeat, and its retention was important if only from the point of view of morale. Joffre finally agreed and gave the orders that the city should be defended to the last man. While making plans for Falkenhayn to fall into his trap on the Somme, he had himself fallen headlong into Falkenhayn's at Verdun.

General Philippe Petain, an exponent of defence, was placed in charge and every inch of ground was contested. Between the time when the first shell landed in February and the end of June when the fighting died away, no fewer than seventy-eight French divisions were fed into the mincing machine of the battle. Verdun smashed the French fighting spirit and brought the French army to the verge of mutiny.

But Falkenhayn's calculations proved only partly right because, while it soon became impossible to convince the French that Verdun was not worth saving, so it also became impossible to convince the Germans that it was not worth taking. The German armies were being slaughtered almost as fast as the French and, in spite of Falkenhayn's pleas for economy and the destruction of Frenchmen by artillery fire, more and more German troops were also fed ruthlessly into the machine. When the fighting died away, the Germans had lost 281,000 to the French 315,000.

Verdun was one of the most insane episodes in a war that Field-Marshal Lord Allenby called bluntly "a lengthy period of general insanity". There was no real prize for either side, though it made Petain's reputation and raised him eventually to the head of the French State. But though Verdun itself could have no great strategic importance either way, it soon began to have its effect on the Battle of the Somme in the growing French resentment against the British. Throughout the long agony of Verdun, Frenchmen everywhere were asking, "Why don't the British help?" As the battle progressed, even the placid Joffre began to show concern and he, too, began to be convinced that it was time the British did some fighting.

As a means of helping, Haig had taken over in March a sector of the French line to relieve troops needed for Verdun, although this had inevitably meant that British troops who should have been resting and preparing for the coming offensive had become involved in the daily drain of trench warfare. Meanwhile, the number of French divisions available for the planned assault on the Somme had shrunk from thirty-nine to eighteen; it had now been accepted that the main blow would have to be delivered by the British and not by the French, as originally intended. This suited Haig, who was by this time convinced that it was his duty to win the war with the forces of the British Empire, and was as anxious as anybody to make a reputation for himself in the field. From his viewpoint, it was obviously better if the French troops took only a minor part in the affair.

–

On May 26th, when the situation at Verdun was looking desperate and the wall-scribblers at home were writing "Strike Now In The West", just as they were to do twenty-five years later before D-Day, Joffre called on Haig and pressed "vehemently" for an early British attack. He lost his temper and claimed that the French army would "cease to exist" if nothing were done until August. As a result of this meeting, July 1st was settled on as a firm date.

Five days later, Poincare, the French President, accompanied by Briand and Joffre, met Haig near Amiens. Present also was General Ferdinand Foch, who was to supervise the French share of the attack on the Somme. So alarmed was Poincare about the state of affairs at Verdun that Haig agreed to bring forward the date of the attack to June 25th, The French demands for help continued all during June.

On the 16th, however, they were beginning to admit that the crisis at Verdun had come to an end and Haig was able to insist on the date of the Somme being set for June 29th, though it was agreed that Foch and General Sir Henry Rawlinson, the commander of the British Fourth Army, which was to make the attack on the Somme, could delay the assault if the weather proved unsuitable.

Meanwhile, the great co-ordinated allied offensive planned at Chantilly had fallen into chaos. In response to Joffre's cries for relief for Verdun, the Italians had promptly made a series of attacks on the Isonzo, which had only allowed the Austrians to break into their rear from the South Tyrol. Before long they, too, were calling for help. This only left the Russians.

In spite of the fact that the ramshackle Russian governmental system was already showing the first signs of the collapse that was to come the following year, two offensives were mounted. But the Germans received full warning of them and they were a failure. When a further appeal came from Italy, the Russians, with no set plan to follow, stumbled on an entirely novel kind of strategy. Without troop concentration, without preliminary bombardments and, as a result, without any warning to the enemy, Brusilov, the commander in the south, launched an attack on June 4th and through sheer surprise succeeded. The Austro-Hungarian front gave way, 250,000 prisoners were taken and a remarkable success was achieved.

Unfortunately, Brusilov had no reserves and, owing to the jealousy of his own colleagues, was given no assistance. His attacks petered out and the Germans struck back. In the end, the Russians paid the price of more than a million casualties. Yet Brusilov's offensive marked the end of real Austro-Hungarian help to Germany. From then on, Austria was kept in the war only by German power. But although the Russian campaign led directly to the fall of the Hapsburgs, it also led directly to the end of the Romanovs.

Perhaps it was the Brusilov offensive that relieved the pressure on Verdun. Certainly, by mid-June, long before the Somme had started, Falkenhayn, studying the mounting German casualties with dismay, had already called a halt to the attacks, and the battle from that point ran down of sheer inanition.

With the end of German pressure on Verdun, the whole reason for the assault on the Somme had been lost. There was no strategical prize involved, and nothing could be gained even by a great advance. The ground had been chosen simply because there the British and the French could fight side by side, but with the French contribution by this time reduced to five divisions, even this point had lost its significance.

It has often been claimed that the Somme was fought to save Verdun, but nothing is further from the truth. The battle had been planned before Verdun started and it is probably nearer the mark to say that the German preoccupation in the south saved the British from even higher casualties than they actually suffered. The Somme did not affect Verdun, except to make the regaining of lost ground easier for the French, though Verdun certainly affected the Somme.

As it happened, Haig, more deeply involved each day with his plans, had come by this time to believe that the war could indeed be won in Picardy. Though the ordinary British soldier also shared this unreasoning faith in a resounding victory, it was not shared by Sir William

Robertson, the Chief of the British General Staff; by Joffre, whose faith lay wholly in attrition; or by Sir Henry Rawlinson, who was to do the fighting.

Yet not a single person suggested calling off the offensive or mounting it in another, more suitable place. In fact, both Robertson and Rawlinson stifled not only their own doubts but also those of their subordinates, and in the end gave their full support to the plan.

Six: All British

The River Somme is a minor waterway in northern France that flows gently through Picardy towards the English Channel. The reeds near the marshy bottomlands are still the haunts of fishermen, and willows and alders fill every valley between the knuckled hills. On the open uplands on either side – wide spaces not unlike the South Downs – there are gentle folds and undulating slopes that contain quiet villages that have changed little since 1870.

The peasants in 1916 were a hard-headed breed who made a good living from their fields and from their orchards. Tall poplars lined the Route Nationale that ran from Amiens to Albert and beyond, straight as an arrow to Cambrai, and under the slopes there were sheltered fields of long grass and hollows warm with the smell of damp earth. Down by the marshy streams, the air was noisy with the cries of water-fowl. On the uplands, however, where the ground was almost solid chalk, water was scarce and supplies had to be carried by cart from pumps and taps. There the farms were constructed like fortresses, of warped beams and baked mud and laths, with the middens in the centre; and dry wiry grass and white flowers like daisies grew along the tops of old walls. With their ancient orchards, fringed with charlock, scabious and cornflower and the inevitable rusting iron crucifixes, the villages – one-street affairs of single-storey buildings – looked poverty-stricken under the wide skies. Only the jerry-built redbrick *Mairies* gave an indication of modernity.

It was a quiet backwater that most people had never heard of, yet it had been fought over a hundred times in previous French wars. Santerre, it was known as – *sancta terra*, sacred land; or perhaps *sangua terra*, bloody land. Charlemagne had lived in Picardy and it had been ravaged by the Normans and the English, by Louis XI and Charles the Bold. It suffered in the Hundred Years War and was Henry V's "tawny ground". The last shot of Napoleon's 1814 campaign had been fired from the walls of Peronne, and the Cossacks who had chased him to Paris had ridden across it. The Germans had crossed it in 1870 and again in 1914. It was fought across again in 1918 and yet again in 1940 and 1944. But it was never more heavily defended than in 1916. As Winston Churchill later observed: "The policy of the French and British commanders had selected for their offensive what was undoubtedly the strongest and most perfectly defended position in the world."

Yet it had been a quiet sector since 1914 and the German defences there had for a long time been neglected. The British High Command, when they took over the sector, changed all that. With their policy of constant activity in the shape of night raids to keep their men on their toes, they not only wasted lives but actually provoked the Germans into strengthening against them the very ground they were planning to attack.

The Germans' four sets of trenches, built by Russian prisoners, had unbroken views for miles over the surrounding slopes beyond the withered wheat and barley abandoned in 1914. By the summer of 1916 the most battle-expert army in the world would have had difficulty in penetrating this position. And Kitchener's Army was far from being that.

Nevertheless, at British Headquarters, optimism as the planning progressed reached such a pitch that common sense began to disappear. There was plenty of heavy artillery – or so it was believed until the attack started – and plenty of shells. The British infantry had an enthusiasm that was unsurpassed in war. There was no need to worry.

Unfortunately, enthusiasm alone can never take the place of experience and this was the one thing the Kitchener battalions did not have. Their training had been rudimentary and they could not operate in scattered bodies, though some of them, when they were allowed to use their initiative, surprised their commanders with their ability. Their officers had been inculcated with the belief that they must obey orders without question and the men had been taught to rely chiefly on the bayonet for killing; even when they arrived in France they were still kept at bayonet practice although experience had long since proved that bombs were far more efficacious. For the most part they had no knowledge whatsoever of trench fighting.

Battalions going into action varied in size because of casualties or the demands that had been made on them. However, usually after leaving details behind, they were about 800 strong and were divided into four companies. Each company, normally about 200 men, was sub-divided into four platoons of about 200 men, and these were again sub-divided into sections of about 12 men.

Haig's headquarters were at Montreuil, fifty miles behind the line, in a chateau where the atmosphere was that of a minor court with military overtones. Haig himself never once visited the front line and neither did his staff, nor did the staffs of the army corps under his command nor, as a rule did the staffs of divisions further down the scale. Headquarters only learnt what it was like at the front in 1917 when General Sir Lancelot Kiggell, Haig's Chief-of-Staff, saw for himself the conditions under which men were having to live. When he did, he was horrified.

But in 1916 it was only at brigade level that it was common for staff officers to go forward to see for themselves, and the leaders on the Western Front all lived well behind the line. Throughout the war they continued to make their plans without any first-hand knowledge of what went on in the narrow blood-soaked strip of ground in front of the Germans. There was practically no liaison between staff and fighting man, and all too often the officers of the staff, on whom so much depended, were men of wealth and family who had been selected less for their skill than for their connections. It was a system that had worked admirably under the Duke of Wellington, but this was the twentieth-century and Haig was no Wellington.

By this time, absorbed with his plans, Haig was being swept along by the offensive, which, at first, he had not wanted. Caught up by his enthusiasm were a slightly bewildered Kitchener, floundering by now in a war of a size that, in spite of his prophetic judgment of 1914, he had never expected; the hard-headed Sir William Robertson, the Chief of Imperial General Staff, who had replaced Kitchener when it had become obvious to everybody that Kitchener's experience was not equal to the task he had taken on; the Prime Minister, Asquith; and finally, Lloyd George, who, although he disliked Haig as much as Haig disliked him, and often said so in private, never had the courage to say so in public.

In view of what had happened in previous offensives, Haig's plan was far too ambitious. While a diversionary attack by two divisions of General Sir Edmund Allenby's Third Army was to draw away German reserves at Gommecourt to the north, the whole German trench system to the south on a twenty-mile front was to be smashed wide open by Rawlinson's Fourth Army, and by part of the French Sixth Army astride the Somme. The breach made, the attacking forces were then to wheel to the north, pushing back the exposed flanks of the enemy, so that Haig's beloved cavalry, under General Sir Hubert Gough, could be sent through the gap and deep into enemy territory. Although the battle was expected to be well contested, Haig thought the initial breakthrough would be made on the first day.

Foch, the leader of the French forces, not only disagreed but also expressed grave doubts about any kind of success at all in 1916. He preached greater concentration of forces before a big attack, but he was overruled, Haig's comment being that "his excuses seemed very lame".

Haig's enthusiasm by this time was running away with him. He was obsessed by the belief that the tremendous artillery barrage he had planned would so smash the enemy's line that the infantry would be able to make their first blow at full force. He was remembering the failures in Flanders in 1915 when there had not been sufficient shelling before attacks or when reserves had not been brought up in time or when the break in the enemy's line had been too narrow. This time, he felt, his plan overcame all these separate difficulties.

Haig was disastrously wrong on the main count, but he did have some ideas on a smaller scale that were sound. He suggested that if the attack did not succeed at once it was to be broken off – though when the time came it was Haig himself who insisted on persisting. He also wanted his troops to start their advance at first light, while it was still difficult to see, but here he was over-ruled by the French who claimed their artillery observers would not be able to watch progress. Two other ideas of Haig's – that there should be only a short bombardment and that small scouting parties should go forward to probe the enemy's defences – were turned down by Rawlinson, who claimed that a short bombardment would not sufficiently cut the wire and that probing attacks were beyond the competence of his New Army soldiers.

Rawlinson, a veteran of Burma, the Nile, South Africa, Ypres and Loos, and a man who could think for himself, had been for some time unhappy with Haig's plan. Privately, says the Official History of the War, he was convinced that it was based on "false premises and too great optimism", for there was no sign that German morale was weakening, and until that happened a decisive success was out of the question. Moreover, he disliked the thought of hurling attack after attack at the enemy. "The trouble is," he said, "this method frequently exhausts the attacker first." He preferred a series of limited attacks with modest objectives, to an attempt at finishing the war in one mighty blow, and in a memorandum, he pointed out the snags in Haig's scheme: the distance the British infantry would have to cover between the German first and second lines; the strength of the fortified villages they would have to face; the strength of the German second line and the difficulty of cutting the wire in front of it; the probability of German reserves arriving before the British reserves; the difficulty of providing support for British troops when they had reached the German second line; and finally the inadequate training of the troops, who were far too green to undertake such a formidable task.

Rawlinson's comments were sound and were proved sound, but in the end, after a long argument, he accepted Haig's plan, just as Haig had accepted Joffre's – though even as late as April 30th, he was writing "I still think we could do better to proceed by shorter steps."

One other commander felt himself in duty bound to disapprove. This was Allenby, two of whose divisions were to make the diversionary attack. Allenby was one of the few great generals of the First World War and might well have been Commander-in-Chief but for Haig's connections. He was a man whose strategy and organisation in the Middle East later in the war were to be faultless. He made his objections clear, suggesting a more effective and less costly subsidiary attack further to the north. Like Foch and Rawlinson, he, too, was turned down.

-

So the plan was finalised. French help had dwindled almost to nothing by now. It was to be a British battle, but Joffre did not withdraw the French altogether because he still had lingering fears that without his men the British attack would never come off, and he gave the plan his blessing.

With everything settled, Haig left for London, where he learned of the death of his supporter, Kitchener. The cruiser, *Hampshire*, which had been taking Kitchener on a pointless errand to Russia, had struck a mine off the Orkneys on June 5th and sunk in heavy seas with practically no survivors.

There was little time for mourning. On the following day, Haig went to Downing Street and got the approval of the War Council for his offensive, and then on to his friend, the King at Buckingham Palace, where he successfully resisted a suggestion that the cavalry should be reduced. While in London, he also met Briand and Joffre, who pressed not only for a start to the Somme offensive but also for a continuation of the Salonika campaign; but he refused to consider any side-show, insisting that all resources in men and munitions should be sent to France.

Joffre's preference for a war of attrition may have begun to affect Haig by this time, however, because at this period he seems uncertain whether he wished for a prolonged battle to destroy the German armies or a tremendous breakthrough to be exploited by cavalry. On June 16th, he wrote: "The advance is to be pressed eastwards far enough to enable our cavalry to push through into open country." And on the 28th, just before the battle started, he was even talking of the quick capture of Bapaume, which was ten miles away and was not in fact captured until nine months later. Yet on the 30th, with the battle about to begin, his Chief Intelligence Officer, Brigadier John Charteris, who ought to have known his intentions, said: "We do not expect any great advance... We are fighting primarily to wear down the German armies and nation..."

Foche and Joffre were puzzled by Haig's ideas, but not over-worried. There were very few French troops involved and any mistakes that were made could be blamed on the British.

Seven: Into battle

Meanwhile, Rawlinson's troops were arriving in France. Some of them were coming straight out from England, fresh, green and inexperienced, still unaware of the potency of French wine and still uneasily conscious of Kitchener's message to troops going on active service: "While treating all women with perfect courtesy, you should avoid intimacy." A few had served in Flanders and were old hands at the game, moving south with the guns through the dusty heat of the summer. For those who had been some months in the trenches, marching was hard on their feet; but the mawkish sentimental tunes – *Tipperary* and *There's a Long Long Trail A-Winding* – carried them along, and now they found it "good to stand on a hill" after the flat plains of the north, and look at scarlet poppies, yellow mustard, clover and cornflowers. After Flanders, the undamaged farmhouses had an air of prosperity and peace, and the rolling folds of Picardy looked exciting after the featureless land of Belgium.

Other troops arrived in the south of France, from the Middle East and the now abandoned

Gallipoli campaign. They were greeted in some cases as saviours and in others – by sour-faced peasants who knew what soldiers, friendly or otherwise, could do – as "*les autres Boches*", the other Germans. They spent their days in trains, cold and often unfed, heads lolling, overcoats and boots undone, trying to pass the time with cards. Occasionally, as they passed a French hospital train moving in the opposite direction, they were appalled by the stench of dirt and decay that spread across stations and sidings, and the cries of "Verdun. Terrible, Tommee, terrible!"

There were brief halts when the crowded men – forty *hommes* or ten *chevaux* to a truck – were allowed out to stretch their legs, but for the most part they were quite unaware of what was going on outside. They could often hear the stamp of horses and at night there would be the flash of torches and the quick jabber of arguments in French; then the crescendo clanking of couplings – bonk bonk bonk – moving back from the buffers until each individual wagon was jerked into motion; then hour after hour again of rumbling along, with pauses and checks without number and endless waits in grassy sidings, until they felt they had "wholly retired from the world".

They began eventually to pass row on row of poplars and grass-covered canal banks, which the travellers among them recognised as the area of the Somme. But still they went on, sometimes passing halted trainloads of Welsh troops, singing hymns in perfect time and harmony, until finally they saw farmhouses and cottages with smashed windows and collapsed roofs and realised that at long last they were approaching the war.

There was a feeling of urgency about Amiens, where many of them detrained. Here and there was the red, white and black crest of Picardy or a speck of horizon blue, or the scarlet-and-gold kepi of a French general. There were hundreds of staff officers about, for Amiens was a boom town making a fortune out of the war. Its restaurants provided excellent cuisines for those who could afford them, and important flagged cars honked their way through the mob.

The men ate their breakfast from cookers parked in the main square in the shadow of the cathedral and began their march to the front, through soldiers sleeping along the streets in hundreds, through horses and guns in such quantities as they had never seen before. They could smell the war now, and see it as it curled about them, ready to sweep them away.

As they marched out, they passed cavalcades of cavalry, magnificent phalanxes of men, flat-capped British with sabres and carbines, and black-bearded blue-turbaned Indians with fluttering lance pennants. The old soldiers jeered. "All they do is pull down all the telephone wires so the infantry have to put 'em up again," they claimed with some truth.

Around them as they marched were men from Bermuda, Newfoundland, New Zealand, Australia, South Africa, Canada, some of them mere boys, some of them wearing medals of long-forgotten campaigns. There were miners from Wales and the Midlands, factory hands from the industrial centres, clerks and shop-boys, ploughmen and shepherds, blond Saxons from the old south-east and swarthy Celts from the west and north, college graduates and dock labourers, men who had come from the far places of the earth where death was not abnormal and men whose chief adventure up to then had been a Sunday afternoon bicycle ride, men from every corner of the British Isles from Devon to Essex, from the Orkneys to the counties of Southern Ireland, wearing the insignias of famous divisions from the Bloody Hand of Ulster to that of the Guards.

The earth was brown with humanity. Every field was full of men and horses, and the arrow-straight road was jammed with wagons and guns and vehicles. Convoy after convoy passed them, rumbling carts with whining axles and square-nosed brass-bonneted Crossley A.S.C. lorries, nose-to-tail; and remounts moving up in twos and thousands of pack mules with tossing heads and wild eyes, trudging from the front, their legs and bellies already caked with the chalky mud of the trenches.

In every village and farm, civilian and military carpenters were at work, hammering bunks together outside barns and sheds. Battery on battery of guns, light and heavy, were ranked in the fields, and thousands of men behind them stacked great piles of shining shells into dumps.

It was exciting and exhilarating. For the first time in the war, Britain was to take the whole burden on her shoulders to relieve the exhausted

French after the vast killing matches of Lorraine, the Marne and Verdun. This time the sausage machine of the old soldiers, fed with men and churning out corpses while remaining firmly screwed in place, was going to be shifted. They couldn't fail. They daren't fail. This was to be the first shaft of sunlight after two years of darkness, the end of sorrow, boredom and pain. They felt a fierce surge of joy that the task had been entrusted to them. This was history and they felt privileged to be part of it.

As they clattered through the cobbled streets of Albert, they saw the first real desolation of the war in broken buildings and empty windows. It was a deserted, shattered, red-brick town where broken chimneys reached for the sky alongside the mined tower of the Basilica. A hundred feet above their heads, the statue of the Madonna and Child hung over them. It had been hit by a shell in the early days of the war and, as legend had it, that if it fell the Germans would win, a French engineer had taken the precaution of strengthening it with a steel cable. Civilians still carried on a makeshift life in the cellars, but there were heavy batteries hidden among the trees and behind the ruined houses.

They marched out of the town to their whining mouth-organs into the Rue de Bapaume, four after four of them, the crunch of their boots muffled by their strong young voices, all of them, rich and poor, stupid and intelligent, reduced to the same drab level, their khaki stained with sweat, their backs chafed by the straps of the equipment, their lips crusted with the white chalk dust, which their moving feet churned up. Overhead, British aircraft buzzed, secure in their superiority, and the men stared eagerly at the lines of observation balloons that hung over the hills, one to every division. Max Immelmann, the German ace, the symbol of German skill, had been killed only a week or two before by 2nd-Lieut. G. R. McGubbin and Corporal H. Waller, flying an old birdcage FE2B, and this fact, too, gave them confidence.

Slowly they moved up to the front. At one village, the writer Robert Graves saw a bright old retired schoolmaster handing out tracts on how to live to be a hundred. "With the Somme offensive," he said, "this seemed to be a good joke." By now the countryside was at its best and squirrels were noticed in the woods near Thiepval, while at Martinsart nightingales kept the encamped men awake.

The marching columns tramped on, their journey often continuing through the night when they could see only hump-backed figures around them and hear muffled voices. Then they began to see faint flickering lights in the sky and hear the dim thudding rumbling of guns, a new sound full of menace, and they knew they had arrived.

They took up their billets in farms and valleys just behind the line, in well-wooded country of sheltered fields and long spring grass and flowers, enduring the discomfort of crowding and the lice that promptly assailed them, knowing that they were there for no other reason than to bring the war to an end.

A few of the newcomers took their place in the line for the sake of experience and were issued with the new bowl-shaped steel helmet, which they joyously pretended to use for every other purpose than the one for which it was intended. Riding up in buses, they entered the vast network of trench systems by a muddy path that gradually sank lower and lower until the surface of the ground was above their heads and they moved in the bones of the earth. The old hands who met them were taciturn, patient men with mud-caked overcoats and unwired caps.

They came to trenches with names like "Piccadilly" or "Princes Street", and began to notice a peculiar sour penetrating smell, compounded of chloride of lime, sweat, manure, and something else that at first they couldn't define – the sickly sweet cloying smell of death. They were staggered to find that the fortifications they'd read of in the papers at home were merely sandbagged holes in the ground, and that dug-outs were only scraped niches covered with corrugated iron, with outside the wry notices put up by bored soldiers, "No Hawkers", "German Bands Prohibited".

They were a little naive and open-mouthed about it all still, shocked by the cynicism of the older soldiers but buoyed up by a sense of duty and patriotism such as had never been seen before and which overcame all the damping effects of the older men's comments.

A turn in the line was invaluable to those who experienced it, for it gave the men an insight into trench fighting. But it was costly in lives because G.H.Q. was still pursuing its policy of raiding. It was part of what the staff called "an active front" – so active, in fact, that between December 1915, and the end of June 1916, more than 125,000 men had been lost in small operations – and was in sharp contrast to the more experienced German and French methods of "live and let live". While it inculcated an aggressive spirit, it placed a great strain on the troops, for there were no quiet sectors where divisions could effectively hold the line and still be resting, and mostly the cost of these "small operations" far exceeded their value and had the opposite to the hoped-for effect on morale.

But the raw troops, wide-eyed and eager, knew nothing of this yet. They were initiated into the mysteries of various enemy shells and bombs nick-named by the old hands "whizz-bangs" and "Jack Johnsons" and "flying pigs". They received their first shocks to the nervous system when their friends were killed, or when they themselves were caught with wiring or raiding parties in No Man's Land by the lash of a searching machine gun, or when the sudden crashes of exploding bombs tore at their senses; and they came out bone-weary, their clothes filthy, their eyes suddenly older, infected a little now by the cynicism of the experienced men and more cautious than they had been before with their lives.

But, for every man who had a chance to see what life in the front line was like, there were thousands who did not, and between the two there was a vast gulf of inexperience. Sir John French and Winston Churchill had urged that the new troops be integrated into the army slowly, gaining experience while still protected by the knowledge of older and wiser soldiers; but Kitchener had always distrusted the new troops and did not wish them to damage old established regiments with their new ideas and their light-hearted attitude to army regulations, and he had had his way.

This very inexperience was one of the chief factors in the tragedy of the Somme.

Eight: Final preparations

The offensive had now reached the final stage of planning, but it was beginning by this time to suffer somewhat from the differing views of Joffre, Haig and Rawlinson.

A frontal assault was to be undertaken once more, in spite of all the previous failures of this type of attack, and since the Germans sat on the heights above the British line, they were able to observe every scrap of the preparations that now commenced. These were so flagrant, in fact, that for a long time the Germans refused to believe they could be for anything but a feint assault, with the main attack being prepared in secret elsewhere.

Yet despite great activity behind the British lines, there were still not enough men for the job to be done, and the troops who were to take part in the offensive had to devote much of their time to digging and carrying supplies. To their disgust, they were rotated between holding the line, labouring and training. There was a vast new army of conscripts growing in England, they argued, who could be brought over to help. Even if the conscripts could not yet fight, they might at least have helped with the backbreaking labour.

For example, since telephone cable was vulnerable to shell fire, it had to be buried; between April 1st and June 30th, the Canadian Corps alone laid 420 miles of metallic circuit six feet deep in its area. Gas was to be used where possible and the heavy containers had to be humped up to the front and dug into the parapets of the jumping-off trenches. Vast ammunition dumps and dumps of stores had to be formed, and great establishments, amounting almost to small towns, had to be constructed behind the lines.

The railways in the area were woefully inadequate, and the roads behind the front were little more than tracks. New railway lines were built – one unit composed chiefly of Yorkshire miners alone spent three months on the job – but, in the belief that the war would soon become one of movement, it was considered wasteful to embark on more than what would be just sufficient for the first days. The same spirit dictated the inadequate road repairs.

Water and at least seven weeks' lodgings for more than 400,000 men and 100,000 horses had also to be provided. Water points were arranged, pumping apparatus – even fire engines – being brought from England, while wells were sunk wherever possible. Accommodation in the scattered villages had to be supplemented by bunks erected in barns, large rooms and huts; and dressing stations, hospitals, prisoner-of-war cages and – more ominously – mass graves were prepared.

During June the area behind the line was a scene of frantic endeavour. On every road were big guns, convoys of lorries, and marching troops, while regiments and divisions practised their share in the assault over dusty ground lined with tapes to represent trenches.

There was something wildly unreal about these mock assaults. The Albert-Bapaume road was marked out with distances, and timings were carefully observed. Staff officers rode about blowing whistles and making notes in between picnic lunches out of hampers. Gas was imagined, blanks were fired and wire was put up.

"Bear in mind," the troops were told, "that the men with flags in front represent the barrage as it moves. Try to imagine that you're carrying your full kit. Try to imagine that you also have wire and bombs and pigeons. Remember your speed must be a steady walk."

Rockets flared and the troops advanced from one crest to the next. But it was all quite unrealistic and hopelessly impractical. They were being taught to advance like the "automata" of Frederick the Great's army, without taking into account that the enemy was no longer armed with muskets but with machine guns. The movements were carried out in silence. Backs were straight. Rifles were at the port, clean, bright and lightly oiled. As Marshal Bosquet had said of the Charge of the Light Brigade, another advance made in much the same manner half a century before, "It was magnificent but it was not war."

All those instructors who were busy telling the infantrymen how to use the bayonet would have been much better employed teaching them to behave as Field-Marshal Lord Wavell recommended in the last war – as a cross between a cat burglar, a poacher and a gangster. And, after two years, it should have been quite clear that advances across No Man's Land under counterfire could never be made in straight lines.

The preparations were made in harassing conditions. There was constant shell fire, which sometimes forced resting battalions out of their billets into the fields to sleep. Fortunately, there was no bombing. As the Royal Flying Corps had complete command of the air, the Germans were unable to send aircraft over.

As the day of the assault drew near, optimism at headquarters grew. Haig had often emphasised in peacetime the tendency in war "to believe what we wish for", but he was now falling into the trap himself. His chief subordinates were telling him exactly what he wanted to hear, with the result that he never attempted to adjust his aims to his reduced resources. Charteris, his Chief Intelligence Officer, was convinced, as late as June 28th, that the Germans had no real idea of any attack in force being imminent. What movement was discovered behind their lines, he interpreted as being that of resting battalions. The Germans, however, made no mistake with their intelligence, and when the Bantam Battalion arrived in the line, they were greeted with shouts of "Cock-adoodledoo". The Welsh Fusiliers heard "You bloody Welsh murderers" and the Royal

Sussex "Bastard Sussekers", while the 12th York and Lancasters from Sheffield were welcomed with queries about their city theatre and were told that the first of them to be captured would be crucified.

Rawlinson was still not convinced about the plan, but at his conferences he was insisting that the bombardment would wipe out everything in front of the attacking men and that all they had to do was walk forward and take possession. This current of optimism spread downwards even to battalion headquarters. But not only were the British far shorter of guns than the French to the south, but their targets were more widely spread.

Moreover, a great many of the brand-new guns and much of the ammunition were defective. In the effort to increase production, standards had been lowered and some of the shells exploded in flight. Others failed to explode at all or blew up in the barrels of the guns, so that the 4.5-inch howitzer batteries became known as "suicide clubs". On July 1st, the troops were to find the ground littered with duds. Lloyd George offered the prompt excuse that the Royal Garrison Artillery was entirely untrained, could not shoot, and was quite unfitted to work "the perfect weapons" he had provided.

The preparations went on. Infantry units without experience were ordered extra training, but now there was neither time nor instructors. It was also suggested that assembly trenches should be dug out in No Man's Land, but in many cases this was not done, and where false trenches were dug to mislead the Germans to the north of the attack area, they were singularly unsuccessful. As one officer said, "the manoeuvre would not have deceived a cadet" and the Germans did not move a single brigade away from the threatened front.

Perhaps the fault was that the British still regarded the war as a bit of a game. There was too much amateurism – even among the professionals. One battery, for instance, who could see the enemy postman, used to try, not to kill him, but to make him drop his letters.

The attack and the diversion were to be carried out in successive waves of infantry along the whole twenty-five miles of front, and the troops had orders to press on at speed to their objectives. Yet little information about mopping up and consolidating captured positions was given by headquarters and the formations to be used inevitably hampered any swift advance. Rawlinson prepared a pamphlet of instructions but although this laid great stress on discipline and on the need for saluting at all times, it made no mention of rifle and machine-gun covering fire or of successful units turning to the assistance of less successful neighbours; and it touched only briefly on the possibility of lightly equipped troops advancing rapidly and on the use of folding ground to cover the advance of small columns. Other commanders, some of whom had never had experience of company or even of battalion warfare, and in some cases were not even infantrymen, gave advice on training and advocated the best methods to be used.

Raids were still being made, though for what purpose apart from stirring up the whole front, it was difficult to surmise. They were hated by the men in the line who regarded them as a useless waste of life; the information gathered from them was of very little value; and nothing was ever discovered of the depth and strength of German dug-outs.

It was just another mistake to add to the growing list.

Nine: The Germans

By this time the Germans were fully aware of the impending attack, though they still could not understand why on earth the British should risk their excellent new armies against what they considered to be the strongest part of their defences. They were certain they had the advantage all along the line. All they had to do was to stay where they were to win the war: the French, they knew, wanted only peace after Verdun.

As early as February, General Fritz von Below, the German commander on the Somme, had suggested that a large-scale attack might take place in his sector during the year, and Crown Prince Rupprecht of Bavaria, a shrewd and efficient army commander, began making notes in his diary about his own position. Very soon the suspicions of these two men became certainties.

A report was sent to Headquarters about the British preparations opposite the fortified villages of Gommecourt and Fricourt, and a preventive attack was considered but abandoned because it was felt the men were more urgently needed at Verdun. But

Von Below still found it hard to believe in an attack, though for the life of him he could not other-wise account for the amount of activity behind the British lines, which was clear to anyone with a pair of field glasses.

On June 15th the German Emperor visited Rupprecht's 6th Army headquarters at Douai just to the north. Von Falkenhayn – who was also present – refused to accept the possibility of an attack on the Somme. Why should the British wish to assault the strongest point in the whole line, he asked. He derided Rupprecht's warning. "The allied offensive will be in Alsace-Lorraine," he claimed, and Von Below was given nothing but a few labour battalions and a few captured Russian howitzers.

But Rupprecht continued to report on the activ-ities behind the French and British lines – the vast increase in rail traffic, the new trenches that were being built, the new artillery sites, the tremendous new camps that were appearing in the country round Albert – and Von Below quietly began to make plans to deal with a possible attack.

With good reason. The belief in an attack that he and Rupprecht had shown had been completely justified. On June 1st, at Sheffield, Christopher

Addison, Parliamentary Secretary to Lloyd George's Ministry of Munitions, had appealed for a postponement of the Bank Holiday, hinting that there was a good reason for it. On the following day at Leeds, Arthur Henderson, Labour Adviser to the Government, in a speech to owners and workers of munitions factories, had also asked for a postponement of the Whitsuntide holidays, saying: "It should suffice that we ask for a postponement... to the end of July. This fact should speak volumes." The speech was widely reported in the London papers and when a copy of it eventually found its way via Holland to Rupprecht's desk, he commented, "It certainly does so speak. It contains the surest proof that there will be a great British offensive in a few weeks."

A British attaché at the Hague, another man who suffered from an inability to hold his tongue, had been heard to say that the offensive was due to begin. This, too, Rupprecht noted. By the 19th of the month, he was convinced the attack was imminent. By the 23rd, he was pretty certain where it was to be delivered and on the next day his theories were confirmed when a British prisoner captured in a raid at Gommecourt gave away the exact date – even the date of the beginning of the great bombardment.

By now even the most sceptical of the German commanders accepted that a major British assault was to be made. Everyone knew it, from Falkenhayn down to the man in the trenches, and Rupprecht noted caustically that the French papers were making much of it. Von Below's demands for reserves were met as far as Verdun would allow.

On June 26th, news of the date came again – this time via the German military attaché in Madrid – and, on the Somme itself, a German pilot, who had managed to fly over the British lines, was able to study the practice of the diversionary attack at Gommecourt, while the following day the German staff worked out the precise number of British divisions taking part from the number of captive balloons they could see. Finally, just to clinch the matter, German listening posts near La Boiselle picked up part of a telephoned order of Rawlinson's, which left them in no doubt about what to expect.

On their own side of the trenches, however, the Germans were careful to maintain the impression of a peaceful and deserted countryside. When British planes flew over, anti-aircraft shells burst in large numbers, but the observers huddled against the wind in the old wood and canvas flying machines, rarely saw a flash from the well-concealed gun positions. They were expert enough, however, to know that the shading that crept along the German reserve trenches showed that the German working parties were active at night even if they were invisible by day. For the shading spelled barbed wire.

Tension grew. The spike-helmeted officers in their hide-outs on the hills saw the dumps and battery sites creep forward. Yet the Germans were not over-anxious. Their positions were excellent. In fact, the water from their trenches, when it had been pumped out the previous winter, had obligingly run downhill and helped to flood the allied positions below.

The ridge where they waited consisted of a series of spurs, the tops of which had been made into fortresses. Woods and villages had also been fortified until they were impregnable, the German engineers working with skill so that an attack anywhere in the vicinity came under cross-fire. Machine gun emplacements were built into the sides of the spurs, often with the weapons concealed in great drainpipes to mask them as they fired. Subterranean passages led to them, and behind, dug-outs thirty and forty feet deep had been built, complete with electric light, washing apparatus, surgeries, hospital wards, bomb-proof cellars and steel railways for the movement of ammunition. All had air and escape shafts and some of the officers' quarters were decorated with cretonnes and had panelled walls. In the rear, old caves and underground passages, dug years before for the quarrying of chalk, were used to shelter reserves.

There were two German lines, each consisting by now of several rows of trenches, and a third one was in preparation; and before each was a formidable belt of barbed wire, sometimes twenty to thirty yards wide, with barbs as thick as a man's thumb and often far too tough to be cut with ordinary wire cutters. On it, like battered scarecrows, hung the remains of old raiding parties.

Although the German front line could be seen, it was impossible to see the second line or its wire entanglement; but the Germans could see everything going on in and behind the British lines. They could even see all four roads leading from Albert to the front and could range their guns on them without difficulty. British attempts at camouflage, like so much else about the British army, were amateurish and consisted chiefly of canvas screens.

The north end of the German line was anchored at Gommecourt, considered to be the strongest fortified position in the whole of France. Just to the south near Beaumont Hamel was another strong fortress, the Schwaben Redoubt, and further south still was the Thiepval Ridge, a commanding position overlooking the Ancre, with the Leipzig Salient and its powerful Hohenzollem Trench.

The other end was anchored by the villages of Ovillers, La Boiselle and Fricourt. In this area were the thick clumps of Mametz, Delville, Trones, Bernafay and High Woods.

Opposite the French, the ground was reasonably flat, but the British would everywhere have to move upwards, with their enemy waiting above – the most depressing way imaginable to start an attack. Knowing this, the Germans sat in their deep dugouts not too troubled by the thought of the coming bombardment. During the past few weeks, they had practised bringing their machine guns and troops up from their shelters in a matter of minutes and, where wire was cut, they simply detailed another machine-gun crew to train their weapon on the gap.

–

To thinking men in the British trenches, looking upwards in the silence of the summer evenings, it was obvious that they had a much tougher nut to crack than the staff had realised.

Haig, however, was confident. He saw nothing to disturb him. His only doubt was about the front of the VIII Corps of General Sir Aylmer Hunter-Weston whom he personally disliked and whose raids had proved singularly unsuccessful. Haig regarded Hunter-Weston and his staff as amateurs, but it was a pity he failed to make searching enquiries into why their raids had failed, and why the young officers, their faces blackened with burnt cork and carrying ladders and bombs, had brought back such ominous reports. In places, the wire had not been cut at all, and the VIII Corps had nowhere been able to break into the German line.

Further to the north at Gommecourt, in the area of the diversionary attack, the British knew they were expected. They wanted to be expected, in fact, so the Germans would move their reserves in that direction. "They know we are coming, all right," said General Sir Thomas Snow to Haig. It was even claimed that in places the Germans had erected notices, "Come on, we're ready for you."

At the last moment, Haig sent Charteris forward to one sector with instructions to stop the attack if he felt there was little chance of success. But the confidence that was bubbling all along the line had infected the commander there and he told Charteris that he "felt like Napoleon before Austerlitz". Charteris permitted the attack to proceed.

There was no suggestion of a delay. In spite of the small things that had gone wrong, it was firmly felt that it would be "all right on the night".

Ten: Moving up

The bombardment opened on June 24th. A tremendous crash of guns set the canvas on the tents in all the camps along the line flapping with the back blast. There was a roar and a flare of flame that sent the camouflage netting leaping in the oven-hot air, then the noise increased and began to ripple and roll all the way along the front from north to south. It was possible to pick out the individual guns as they went off – the ear-splitting bark of the 18-pounders, the cough of the howitzers, and the reverberating crash of the heavy guns away in the rear. As the first tremendous explosion settled down to a jerky roar, shirt-sleeved men came to the doors of their tents and stared to the distant hills where they could see rolling clouds of smoke, and any doubts and fears that had started in their minds over the past weeks dropped away again under the rolling iron-throated thunder.

Beyond the hills, the bombardment continued, rattling over the hot damp valleys like the fluttering of gigantic wings, like some iron monster that would soon snatch up all the thousands of men, all the guns, all the animals, all the machinery, and fling them into the final holocaust that would end the war. The offensive seemed suddenly to have coiled itself together like some tremendous beast about to spring.

In the bombardment, more than a million and a half shells were flung at the German lines, culminating in a hurricane of explosives just before the assault. To the Germans, even though they were expecting it, the shock was appalling. They had never had to endure such a bombardment before, and they were deafened by the noise and stifled by the fumes of the explosions. Even before the assault, hundreds of Germans were suffering from shell-shock, and those troops who were sent up from the deep dug-outs to man the trenches until the attack came considered their duties not far short of suicide.

To the waiting British, however, it was all tremendously exciting – as one of them said, "like the sound of the whole British Empire getting into battle" – and they cheered every big explosion, which they felt was making their job easier.

Yet although the German positions were badly damaged, the German counter-batteries, waiting to blast the attack to shreds when it came, were rarely hit. Low clouds and heavy showers hampered Royal Flying Corps reconnaissance, and many of the observation officers of the heavy batteries had arrived too recently to have had a chance to study the land. Moreover, some of the heavy battery crews had had as little as eleven weeks' training. The lighter guns were having hardly any effect at all, and it soon became clear that there were still not enough guns by a long way to swamp the enemy as had been intended.

In spite of the tumbled stakes and corkscrew supports of the entanglements, the wire was not being cut.

–

Meanwhile, for the British infantry, unaware that the bombardment was not succeeding in its purpose, there was a sense of elation as they put their kits together. Every man's helmet was marked with a divisional sign, and shoulder straps were tied with ribbons to indicate their owner's company. In addition, regimental devices were sewn beneath the backs of collars, and squares of tin attached to packs so that aircraft, searching for the forward troops in the battle, would catch the glint of the sun on them and know where they were.

There was a great deal of excitement and improvised cricket matches took place. The sentimental and patriotic ballads sung around the fires turned into impromptu concerts that ended with the rough young voices singing *Auld Lang Syne* and *God Save The King*. Underneath all the tension as the final preparations were made and the soldiers gathered their belongings together there was an extraordinary politeness between the men and a strange gentleness in the way they treated their friends.

On the evening of the 27th, thousands of little fires burned in the darkness in the hollows where the Germans could not see them. Because sleep did not come easily, groups of men sat up late, singing softly and nostalgically over the reedy chant of mouth-organs. The water birds called from the streams, and the nightingales in the woods – "them bloody sparrers" the troops called them – seemed louder than ever. A few men played cards, others rested against trees, surrounded by scraps of paper – letters from home, which had been torn up so that no man should have about him anything that might identify his unit. Over the horizon the bombardment still thumped and thudded and rumbled, the flashes lighting up the sky as the last letters home were written, often by candlelight under groundsheets where naked lights were forbidden.

Everything was ready. Messages had been read to the men and, in some brigades, ceremonial parades had been held with flags and drums and a march past. Provost police had taken up positions – quite unnecessarily – to deal with deserters.

The movement started forward on June 28th, the rear troops moving through the choked, battered streets of Albert where the Hanging Virgin on the Basilica gleamed at every gun flash, then tramping forward again to the turning-off points. A few villagers appeared at their doors to watch, and in one village the cure stood by the iron calvary at the end of the street, sombre in black soutane and shovel hat, raising his hand in blessing as they passed.

The whole front seemed to be on the move past the route signs and the guides and the flags – horse-drawn wagons and caterpillar tractors, even still the occasional gun; ambulances and steam-engines; and tremendous columns of men flowing towards the sun, singing as they went, all touched with the same bright faith in victory. There was something splendid about these young men. They were the pick of their towns and villages, and every one of them was a volunteer – the first to volunteer. They were inspired by love of country and a conviction that human freedom was being challenged by military tyranny. They didn't grudge the sacrifice or shrink from the ordeal as they marched forward to fulfil the high purpose of duty.

The air was full of petrol fumes and the smell of warm oil, and the sickly sweet scent that was the lingering aroma of gas shells. The tramp of boots and the grinding of wheels were interrupted incessantly by the clatter of hooves as columns of mules went by loaded with ammunition, or a cloud of lancers moved up for the break-through.

Although the movement went well, there were inevitable delays, and the men were soon exhausted. They were carrying a frightful weight of equipment. They had filed past various dumps, picking up shovels and picks and wire, or corkscrew stakes or bombs or water or pigeons. Yet every man was already in what Headquarters considered to be "fighting order", the suitable rig-out to kill enemies or to defend himself in hand-to-hand fighting in a crowded trench. This on its own included a steel helmet, an entrenching tool, a rolled groundsheet, a water bottle, a haversack containing shaving gear and extra socks, the unconsumed portion of the day's rations and extra cheese, special emergency rations, two gas helmets for the different types of gas they might expect, goggles in case of tear gas, wire-cutters, field dressings and iodine, two sand-bags and 220 rounds of ammunition. In addition, they were now loaded with all they had picked up in the dumps as they passed, the flares, the sacks of extra bombs, and the wire. The men of one battalion even carried large sausages by their sides to supplement their rations. With rifle and pack, water-bottle and mess-tin, and without any of the extras, their kit weighed 66 lbs and made it impossible to move at any pace quicker than a slow walk.

Eleven: Before zero

Slowly the great weight of men moved forward, carrying their home-made flags and slogans, passing through now-deserted villages where the walls were daubed with divisional signs and messages – "Now for Berlin" and "Look Out, Kaiser Bill". Outside the empty billets, more torn letters fluttered.

About midday on the 28th, it began to rain in torrents and they were drenched in a moment, while the surface of the dusty roads changed to a white pasty chalk-mud, which was to become only too familiar in the weeks to come. Then, in confusion and without explanation, they were drawn off the road and told to make shelter for themselves wherever they could get it, in ruined barns and houses and under groundsheets in dripping copses.

Owing to the weather, the attack had been postponed for two days until July 1st and the bombardment on these unscheduled extra days slackened, particularly from the heavy guns, which were the ones that mattered. With the offensive wound up to begin, those men who had already taken over from the machine gun, mortar and reserve companies holding the assault trenches, had no chance of being relieved. For forty-eight hours, soaked, miserable and hungry, they had to stay in their flooded positions, nervously checking their equipment, going over their orders again and again, trying to prepare a little warm food whenever they could.

Now that the attack was imminent the Germans did not hesitate to unmask their batteries and reply to the shelling, and in many cases the men in the forward areas were forced into the open by the shells, often receiving heavy casualties. Clinging to every bit of shelter they could find, they began to long for zero hour.

It was while they waited that the last raids were mounted. In some places, however, the Germans lay low in their trenches and the silence caused everyone in their area to believe that the bombardment had plastered them into the ground. Along most of the line, it was firmly believed that the fortifications opposite had been reduced to a litter of shell-holes and that machine-gun emplacements and observation posts had been smashed to rubble.

A few of the more discerning commanders were less sure and sent final patrols to find out. The reports they sent back varied. Two groups from the 29th Division opposite Beaumont Hamel reported the enemy line "not much damaged", while two others in the same area reported it "very much damaged". In one regard, however, they were all agreed. The wire was still there, hardly touched. In front of Gommecourt and Thiepval, in fact, it appeared to be intact. One other thing the raiding parties discovered to their horror – there were far more machine guns opposite them than they had expected. One Divisional headquarters' reply – made from the security of a safe dug-out behind the line – was merely that the men making the report were "windy".

On the night of the 30th, the movement from the rear into the jumping-off trenches started again, and the men up in front settled down to endure a little longer. Those behind pushed to their places in the crowded ditches through the mist hanging about the hollows, that made the knuckly hills stand out like islands in a pearly sea, and dripped off the brims of helmets and eyelashes and clung to the down on cheeks.

As they moved forward, roots and telephone wires snagged against equipment and entrenching spades, which, in some cases, were worn in front in the hope that they might stop a fatal bullet. Already the men were plastered with chalky mud and bone-weary, and now they began to come across victims of the growing German counter-fire, heaps of twisted rags muttering and groaning, and groups of dead men, blackened butchered bodies on the firestep or on the wooden duckboards at the bottom of the trench, most of them still uncovered. As they settled in, they cleared the corpses away, pushing them up on to the parapet behind them, thankful to have something to do, and all the time as they worked a steady stream of wounded straggled back, all of them complaining of the strength of the German shell-fire. In front of them the noise was growing and big shells had set fire to villages behind the German positions that sent thick columns of smoke into the sky.

The exhausted men crouched in their congested trenches, unable to rest. They still retained their faith in ultimate victory but were longing now to have it all over and done with, if only to bring to an end all the hateful waiting and all the wretched humping of loads.

German shells were banging away viciously now at the front line and those in support could see the smoking clods of earth flung up, and the showers of stones and twists of smoke. There were occasional shouts of "Foul" and "No ball" but they were a little forced and no longer considered funny.

Some of the men among the waiting troops, as the light increased, must have realised that this would have been the moment to go in to the attack, instead of later when the sun would be well up. But there was still some time before the scheduled hour, and they had to continue to wait in the litter of ruined ramparts, watching the rats leave. These fat old-stagers, who had been there since 1914 feeding on the dead, now seemed to sense that something was about to happen.

The uneasy rumours about uncut wire began to filter through, and men with periscopes peered anxiously over the waving grass and poppies and charlock and scabious. But No Man's Land still looked like a meadow, full of insects and warmth, and all they could see of the Germans was a low broken ridge of sandbags and wire, and the white reserve trenches herring-boning the hillside.

There was still a mist in the hollows as the larks got up. One or two of them came into the trenches, perching on the trussed and blanketed bodies of the dead, apparently a little dazed by the bombardment, and it was possible to catch them. Men were cleaning rifles, muttering prayers, every man isolated in his own little oasis of loneliness, each waiting with a different set of fears and hopes for the sun to get up, throat dry and stomach twisted with apprehension.

Twenty miles behind the line, Sir Douglas Haig was still asleep. Before going to bed, he had written to his wife: "I feel that every step in my plan has been taken with divine help." To his diary he had confided: "The weather report is favourable for tomorrow. With God's help I feel hopeful. The wire has never been so well cut."

He had visited his corps commanders and claimed that one and all were full of confidence, a statement that did not entirely agree with what the generals themselves thought. Rawlinson, at least, still considered the attack "a gamble", and even Charteris, who for months had been telling Haig what he wanted to hear, thought they were embarking on a long and weary battle. Haig, however, expected to reach the second German line on the first day and with a little luck achieve the breakthrough he so dearly wanted. But many old soldiers in the trenches had their doubts as they studied the bare undulating ground in front of them.

—

With dawn on July 1st, the final bombardment began. Just before it started, several men noticed, a vast hush fell over the battlefield. Thanks to air supremacy, there was not a German aircraft in sight. The mist in the marshes, although it made observation difficult, gave promise of a glorious day.

Then at 6.25 the final roar of the guns came.

A lieutenant of the Royal Field Artillery, who had moved up to an observation post in the front line, said that the boom of the heavy guns swelled to a jerky roar that was flung from horizon to horizon, like thunder tossed from mountain to mountain. "It seemed to throb in our veins," he said. "And then, at last, ten minutes before zero, the guns opened their lungs ... For a mile, stretching away from me, the trench was belching forth dense columns of white, greenish and orange smoke. It rose, curling and twisting, blotting everything from view. It seemed impossible that men could withstand this awful onslaught … And yet a machine gun played steadily all the time from the German front line."

A soldier with the 22nd Manchester said: "The air seemed to be full of a vast and agonised violence, bursting now into groans and sighs, now into shrill screaming and pitiful whimperings, shuddering beneath terrible blows, torn by unearthly whips … It did not begin, intensify, decline and end. It was poised in the air, a stationary panorama of sound, a condition of the atmosphere, not the creation of man." The noise of the bombardment could be heard in England and they said afterwards that even the worms were dead in the ground of the shock.

The air rocked and quivered and the trenches where the troops waited seemed to heave and shudder. It was awe-inspiring and gave them confidence and they began to shout as they compared watches and adjusted straps and gripped sandbags, wire and all the rest of the paraphernalia they'd been given. They began to laugh, drunk from the din.

Then, as the salvos shredded the curling smoke and mist, scarlet star-shells burst in the air above the German line and slowly curved towards them, and immediately shells began to fall on them as the counter-bombardment increased. On one part of the front line, gas containers that had been dug into the parapets were shattered. Owing to lack of wind, the decision had been taken in all but one division not to use gas, but the containers were still there and in one gas unit, fifty-eight men out of sixty-four became casualties to their own equipment.

The banging of shells came closer and showers of dirt and stone began to fall in the British lines with the peppery reek of high explosive. As the curtain of fire came down, the men flung themselves into the bottom of the trenches, cowering awkwardly under their equipment, struggling to dig out friends who were buried as trench walls bulged and erupted. Already, with the lines long since cut, it was impossible to keep in telephonic communication with Brigade Headquarters. Above them the sun was burning bright, laying a line of gold along the top of the parapet where the machine-gun bullets from the German trenches began to cut the grass and snip off the poppy heads and send little glissades of dirt into the trenches. One quartermaster sergeant-major who had arrived with a last-minute consignment of boots for his men watched the Germans expertly shooting the old boots off the parapet as he put them there out of the way.

Just before zero, the mortars joined in. The order was given, "Fix bayonets." Mines went off to add to the deafening row. One under the Hawthorn Redoubt at Beaumont Hamel, which was held by the German 119th Reserve Regiment, contained 45,000 lbs of ammonal. The commander of the VIII Corps had wished to fire this mine four hours before zero, feeling that it would catch the Germans in their trenches, but Haig, on the advice of the Inspector of Mines, forbade it. As it was, the explosion blocked neighbouring dug-outs and the ground all round was white with chalk debris as though it had been snowing. Unfortunately, these mines, constructed by men often working stripped to the waist in primitive conditions, were far too scattered to be of any value and acted only as a warning to the Germans.

In the British trenches, men swallowed nervously and shook hands. It was seven-thirty. The barrage lifted and there was a strange uncanny silence for a few seconds.

Then, as the whistles went, a hundred thousand men scrambled up the ladders and into the open, forming up as they had been told, in straight lines, at a correct distance from their neighbours, their rifles at the port, their heads up as though on parade. Clean, bright and lightly oiled.

Twelve: July 1st

The official dates of the Battle of the Somme are from July 1st to November 18th, 1916, and in spite of the many strange and terrible things that occurred during these months, the most terrible of all was still that first day, a day of perfect summer weather, which witnessed the worst defeat suffered by British arms since Hastings.

Fifteen British divisions from six army corps went forward together. The men threaded their way through the British wire and took up their positions in front. Those in the rear trenches, or those with more experienced officers, had already left their shelters before the German counter-barrage came down and lay in No Man's Land waiting for the signal to advance. Then, as the whistles went, they rose to their feet.

Automatically, at the given moment, the barrage had moved on to the German second line. It was too late now to countermand any orders. The magnificent new armies of civilian soldiers, arranged by their generals in a formation that made a perfect target, began to head towards the German trenches.

One important lesson of Verdun – the most important perhaps had been overlooked: the amazing resilience of flesh and blood under fire. It had been too easily assumed that the complete obliteration of the enemy's fortifications meant also the obliteration of the enemy's spirit. "We relied," said one commander, "far too much on our artillery not only pulverising the hostile works, which it did – but also on its maiming or cowing into inertia all the defenders of each trench line in succession, which it did not." The troops began their slow unrealistic tramp forward. Many carried home-made banners as signs of their enthusiasm, and advanced almost as though it were a sporting event, kicking footballs and cheering. The little copses ahead of them, which, the day before, had been thick growth, were now blasted bare of leaves and, as the shells of the German counter-barrage came closer, clods and stones were flung whining into the air, and the smoke puffs looked "for all the world like a clump of trees suddenly sprouting from the earth".

One N.C.O., who had been worrying that his nerve would not sustain him through the coming ordeal, now noted that he felt quite happy and self-possessed. He went forward with the rest of his company, and a man beside him commented: "If it's all like this, it's a cake-walk."

But the German line, although severely damaged by the British barrage, was by no means mined and the German artillery, not much hurt, was able to concentrate on stopping the infantry. It soon became clear to the advancing men that something had gone horribly wrong. Already they were being cut down by the flying shards of steel from exploding shells. And now the German machine gunners were beginning to emerge with their weapons and take up positions on the shattered parapets and even out in No Man's Land, in full view of the advancing British moving towards them across, in some places, a thousand yards of open ground.

A German soldier in the Schwaben Redoubt has described how he could see masses of British steel helmets – a series of extended lines of infantry – as the machine guns were dragged into position. The first line, which appeared to continue without end to right and left, was quickly followed by a second line, then a third and a fourth, advancing quietly as though at manoeuvres. "They came on at a steady pace as if expecting to find nothing alive in our trenches," he said.

When the first line was within a few hundred yards, emerging from the smoke of the barrage, the order to fire was given and the rattle of machine guns and rifles broke out along the whole line of shell-holes.

Coming through the grass with a strange chirping sound, the bullets cut furrows in the ground and, as the range was found, the lines, still advancing at a steady walk in spite of the instinctive urge to hurry, still upright, still carrying their rifles at the port, began to melt away. Men simply rolled forward slowly to lie on their faces, their knees bent under them in a posture of prayer. As the survivors approached the German wire, they saw to their horror that only a few stakes had been uprooted. Instinctively they drew together at the gaps, still flinching from the cracking shells that covered them with dirt and the blood of their friends, and it was there that the criss-cross streams of bullets caught them again. The bobbing line of helmets thinned away to nothing.

"Whole sections seemed to fall," reported the German soldier, "and the rear formations, moving in close order, quickly scattered. The advance rapidly crumbled under this hail of shells and bullets. All along the line men could be seen throwing up their arms and collapsing, never to move again."

The only things that might have redeemed the unrealistic plan were surprise and speed, but these had been firmly set on one side. The French had resisted all efforts to start the attack at dawn and the troops were so laden with their equipment they could only move forward at a slow plod. Yet they continued to advance, struggling to keep their formation, blinking and wincing at the fire, each wave 100 yards apart; and they fell in rows, sometimes not more than a few paces from their own trenches.

The second, third and fourth waves, following behind, crossed the first British trench, with its tumbled sandbags and sprawled corpses lying in shell holes, in groups "like fish in a basket". As they entered No Man's Land, they began to come across the remnants of the first wave, which had disappeared into the smoke ahead of them, lying in thick swathes, as if they were corn cut down by a scythe, a few of them still moving awkwardly or trying to crawl with horrifying clumsiness to the rear. At the wire, they came across more bodies lying in heaps in the openings, like skittles knocked over in a giant game, whole rows of them, dead where they had fallen, and whole masses more heaped against the outside fringe, scarecrows with their arms spread-eagled, their clothes caught by the barbs as they fell, some of them burnt to death by primitive flame-throwers. Then they, too, were hit by the blast of the machine guns and melted away themselves like smoke.

Those artillery observers in a position to watch the advance could not believe what they saw. "I thought they were all lying down because of the fire and would get up again," one of them said. To their horror, it began to dawn on them that all the khaki figures sprawled in rows before the German lines were dead.

–

Only where a few individual commanders ignored orders did they manage to penetrate the German line. Brigadier-General J. B. Jardine, in command of the 97th Brigade opposite the Leipzig Salient, an officer who had been attached to the Japanese Army in the Manchurian War, was aware of what machine guns could do, and had had his men creep forward in his sector to within thirty to forty yards of the German line. They were in the enemy trenches within two minutes and the defenders were taken prisoner before they could emerge from their dugouts.

But just to the north, Crozier, advancing with the Belfast Battalion of the Royal Irish Rifles, saw rows upon rows of British soldiers lying dead, dying or wounded. In spite of the bursting shells and smoke, which made visibility poor, he could see "heaped-up masses of British corpses suspended on the German wire in front of the Thiepval stronghold, while live men still rushed forward in orderly procession to swell the weight of numbers in the spider's web".

Men were falling "like human cornstalks" and, partly due to their patriotic zeal and spirit of self-sacrifice, which led them to go on trying long after it had become impossible to advance, the casualties of the British troops were enormous. Units that had gone over cheering were soon reduced to nothing more than huddled disorganised groups, their numbers decimated. Some battalions had lost all their officers and most of their men in the first hour of the attack. Their training had been insufficient and they did not grasp the need for rapid independent action at moments of crisis. When senior officers fell dead, juniors, through lack of experience, were unable to take their places, and when subalterns fell, the N.C.O.s who had to assume command often knew little more than the rank and file.

Louis Mairet, a Frenchman, summed it up when he said they "lacked savoir-faire", and the Germans took full advantage of this lack of know-how and were seen, idiotically brave on occasion, standing on their parapets to fire, often within 150 yards of the British.

Only occasionally did little groups of desperate wild-eyed shocked soldiers manage to reach the German front line, but there were rarely enough of them to consolidate their gains. Because they had been told to press on to their second objectives and because they thought it was their duty, a few of them tried, going inevitably to their deaths. But for the most part even the most successful got no further than the first trench, a tangle of shell-holes that was no longer recognisable as a fortification. There were desperate hand-to-hand encounters with equally shocked Germans emerging from the smashed entrances to their dug-outs, dreadful affairs of club and bayonet in congested holes where the living tripped over the dying, until suddenly, a few demoralised men, drunk with shock and horror and covered with blood, found themselves in possession of an unspeakable ditch littered with the bone-white bodies of the dead. But though they had succeeded, they were now unable to ask for the help they needed to consolidate their gains. They were beyond help. Once they had passed through the curtain of shell-fire they were as effectively cut off as if they had never existed. All communication with the rear had gone.

As they turned, looking for the reserves they confidently expected to support them, they saw the following lines advancing like driven partridges before the guns. Here and there they could hear bugles and drums or the skirl of bagpipes through the smoke, but the Germans were recovering rapidly now, and more and more machine guns were being dragged up. The reserve lines crumpled up just as the first had done, until there was nothing left except a few isolated figures standing almost stupidly in the long grass, "like calves smelling blood".

Only after the long waves of men were destroyed was any real progress made. Then primitive cunning reasserted itself against the authorised tactics and small groups under some natural leader worked their way forward. In many places, however, the failure to mop up the Germans in sections of captured trench enabled the Englishmen to be taken in the rear and destroyed as they passed on to the second objectives. And even when it was obvious that further advance was impossible, supporting troops, because of the lack of contact with the rear and because of the dearth of skilled commanders, were still allowed to go forward to suffer the same fate as the first waves.

The Ulster Division had made a deep penetration near Thiepval, but it was never consolidated because their corps commander, Sir Thomas Morland, had used up his reserves against an impossible strong-point elsewhere, and because he had forbidden commanding officers, seconds-in-command and adjutants or representatives of Brigade HQ to be with the advancing battalions. The result was that there was no one to co-ordinate the efforts of the troops, and only in a few cases did commanding officers such as Crozier ignore orders and remain with their battalions to direct their men.

Fricourt, in the right centre, formed a turning point, however. To the south, trivial gains were made by XIII Corps, under General W. N. Congreve, V.C., but not without heavy casualties. But below the River Somme, on a front of nearly eight miles, the French achieved their objectives. They had held back until 9.30 a.m. and the Germans, not expecting anything from them after Verdun, had given up waiting. Lieut-Col. B. C. Fairfax, commanding the right-hand British battalion, and Commandant Le Petit, the commander of the French regiment on his right, had stepped over the parapet with the second wave at the point of junction and led the advance arm-in-arm.

Foch's men – the famous Iron Corps who had been through the mill of Verdun – marked up a real success. Following an overwhelming bombardment, they moved forward not in long lines but in small groups as they had learned in the great battle to the south, taking advantage of a river mist and the folds of the ground, each group giving covering fire to its neighbours. They advanced with great tactical skill, and overran the German front line with comparatively light casualties.

All to the north, however, where the old-fashioned principle of surprise had been put aside, there was nothing but failure. Back in the British lines, reports and rumours kept arriving. Within three hours, Hunter-Weston was faced with the bitter decisions of defeat, though the size of the disaster opposite Serre and Gommecourt was still not fully known. To artillery officers in their observation posts information had come that the front line opposite had been taken without resistance, that Beaumont Hamel had fallen, and that the enemy were giving themselves up in hundreds, but by 11.30, when the smoke cleared, not a movement could be seen. Serre, originally hidden by thick trees and hedges, now stood bare and shattered, its trees leafless "as though a comb had been dragged through them". Later, the full truth became known. As the infantry came running back the Germans stood up, unmolested, and shot them down. Those who survived, when asked where their companies were, replied, bitterly: "Hanging on the wire."

In the confusion, friend and foe alike were fired on. Crozier, with the Ulsters, saw an advancing crowd of field-grey soldiers falling before the firing like grass before a sickle, and only then realised they were not counter-attackers but prisoners, escorted by British wounded. At another point he was confronted by a group of shattered soldiers, utterly demoralised and straggling to the rear, who were turned back by a young subaltern drawing his revolver and shooting one of the party.

Crozier was cut off for days, torn, filthy, using a thirty-foot deep dug-out for a first-aid post and headquarters combined. By nightfall of July 1st, the place "was like a madhouse". It had originally been full of dead and wounded who had had to be cleared, and now wounded men, delirious with pain after lying in the broiling sun all day, or dazed and shocked by shell-fire and the death of their comrades, kept coming in. The birds they had heard that morning had gone. Thiepval was masked by a wall of corpses and Thiepval Wood had vanished. By the time he retired, Crozier had seventy men left out of 700.

The tally of prisoners indicated the extent of the failure. The most successful corps took only 934, the least successful only 22. Divisions had been thrown back by mere regiments and the British losses in men were irreplaceable.

–

Throughout a day of blazing beauty, surrounded by scarlet poppies and cornflowers, the shocked British troops, their clothes torn by the wire, clung to shell-holes out in No Man's Land or to the rare fragments of the German line they had managed to capture. All round them were the heaps of the dead but no sign of life except occasional groups of running figures trying to get back to their own trenches. Scattered among the long grass was the debris of the attack, the punctured water cans, the baskets with the dead pigeons, the rolls of wire and the torn earth.

In the stifling heat of the afternoon, they tried to comfort their wounded with water taken from the dead, while the flies descended in their millions to make life more wretched for those who survived and were hanging on, praying for night. Then, as it grew dark, No Man's Land seemed to come to life, with wounded men rising like ghosts and slowly crawling out of the dips and hollows and making their painful way back.

The Germans were still firing flares and there was still occasionally the rattle of machine guns or the tap of rifles as the men slipped thankfully into the British trenches, some of them looking "as though they'd been buried and dug up again". The unwounded brought in the wounded and went out again and again to bring in more, until the front trench was cluttered with dead and dying.

All the time the British front was in a state of nervous tension in case the Germans, taking advantage of the disaster, should counterattack. But the Germans never came. In spite of the British catastrophe, the Germans had been hurt, too, and in some areas had even brought up batmen, cooks, clerks and storemen to man the line. That night, though, in the confusion, they could, if they'd wished, have walked straight into the British positions.

Men stumbled in as long as darkness lasted, calling out the names of their units or their friends, and sat weeping on the broken firestep where they had formerly stood to stare over the parapet, while doctors and padres with martyred faces attended to the wounded and the dying. And out in the hollows in No Man's Land the remains of those tremendous waves lay in piles that were sometimes four feet high, still with the home-made flags that proclaimed their enthusiasm and their faith and their exaltation, while all around them the flayed earth was covered with scrap-iron – shards of shell cases, spent bullets, bomb splinters and shrapnel balls. Seeing it afterwards, "it was amazing to think men had got as far as they had".

When daylight came, the Germans in some parts of the front, particularly in the north where the casualties were heaviest, raised white flags and moved among their own wire attending to the British wounded. The gesture developed into an informal truce with Red Cross flags, though the Germans made no secret of removing Lewis guns on the stretchers along with the bodies and refused to permit British medical men near their positions.

Already the ugly name of Gommecourt was filtering through. There had never been any intention of tactical gain being made in that area and there had been no attempt at concealment. The attack had been a forlorn hope from the start and disaster there was complete. But Gommecourt was not alone. There were other places, too, where success had been expected – Serre, for instance, where there was nothing to show for 14,000 casualties, and Fricourt, where the machine guns had accounted for 8,000 dead and wounded, and a dozen other places. The Irish near Thiepval had smashed through four sets of trenches but were now isolated and beyond help. The Newfoundlanders had been wiped out at Hamel and the South Wales Borderers at Beaumont. The Durhams had been decimated at Ovillers and the Green Howards at Fricourt, and the York and Lancasters at Serre. Whole battalions, thousands and thousands of men, had been swept away in an unbelievable butchery in the first few minutes after 7.30, and behind the line where the counter-barrage had fallen, hundreds more bodies lay about like pieces of wreckage, the salvage parties moving among them collecting their rifles and bombs, while the Pioneer Corps, who should have been repairing captured trenches, were set to work with artillerymen and engineers to bury the dead and clear away the wounded.

One man, surrounded by corpses, described a loud wailing "as if huge wet fingers were being dragged across an enormous glass pane, rising and falling, interminable and unbearable", that came from a muddy sunken road where hundreds of wounded were shouting, moaning, and singing in delirium.

The woods behind the lines were now nothing but brushwood with every tree cut off at the top to add to the impenetrable tangles that sliced the sun into dusty beams. They were binned and scorched by shell-fire and, on the fringes, dead men and horses and mules lay about among smashed wagons and guns that showed where the German artillery had done its deadly work.

Even the birds seemed to have vanished from the awful charnel house of the Somme. All the way back from the front, along the route to the rear, stiffening bodies filled the ditches and wounded men sat by the roadside, wearing turbans or body belts of bandages, going through the dumb, stupefied, mechanical actions of exhaustion and pain.

Almost 60,000 men had become casualties, 20,000 of them killed. Most of the missing were dead, because few prisoners were taken.

"Papa" Joffre had had his way. The British army had been "involved".

So appalling were the losses on that July day that the official historian had difficulty in forming a detailed account of the fighting. Regimental diaries were in most cases scant and even non-existent. In some instances, not a single unwounded officer could be traced. By comparison, Alamein – never considered an easy battle – cost only 13,500 in twelve days of hard pounding.

Yet Haig's chronicler, Colonel Boraston, had the nerve to write that the day bore out the conclusions of the British Higher Command and amply justified the tactical methods employed.

July 1st was, however, not just a wanton pointless carnage. It was also an epic of heroism that proved the moral quality of Kitchener's men. In spite of everything, these untried battalions remained unbroken – even with casualties not believed possible in undestroyed units. They carried on for almost five more months and, notwithstanding their inexperience, actually came within measurable distance of breaking the German line.

Thirteen: "Press on!"

After this disastrous start, it is difficult to understand why Haig, contrary to his own declared intentions, persisted in the attack. Perhaps the bulldog element in his character did not permit him, once he had taken a bite into the German line, to let go. Or, perhaps more simply, it was because so much had been expected and so much boasting of success had been done that it was impossible to think of breaking off the fight.

True enough, commanders behind the front had been rendering reports far more rosy than the few facts in their possession warranted and were still telling Haig what he hoped to hear. No thought of failure entered anyone's head and the spotless divisions of cavalry still waited for the gap through which they were to charge. Charteris thought there were now only three much-harassed German divisions in reserve, an opinion that seemed even to the *Times* correspondent, Colonel Repington, "an extraordinary hallucination".

Charteris's figures were so artificial, in fact, that Rawlinson did not "consider the casualties excessive". He was not aware, of course, that there had been, not 16,000 casualties out of 100,000, as he believed, but 60,000, an appalling figure considering that it included almost no prisoners. Even so, with what little information he had, Haig was beginning to see the situation more clearly on the second day, when he was moved to comment: "The news was not altogether good."

Confronted with a difficult situation, he did not decide until July 2nd to push hard in the south where he had achieved a measure of success, but by then, though he had plenty of reserves, ammunition for the guns was beginning to run short.

By night-time on July 1st, however, the Fourth Army was still continuing its attack. The impetuous Gough, the man most fitted by temperament to lead the surge forward after the breakthrough was given the unenviable task of taking over the two shattered northern corps. When he arrived, he found there was not the slightest possibility of carrying out what he called Rawlinson's "light-hearted orders to renew the attack next morning", as between them these two corps had suffered 20,000 casualties. He wisely stopped the forward movement of men.

But Gough was only one. In other sectors the reserves were still trying to press forward, hampered by the wounded streaming back and the debris of the battle that littered every route, unable to advance much even in the areas where there had been some success. With every shell that dropped on the German lines, with every step forward they took, the harder it grew to advance. The railway was fast to deliver men to the battlefield, but once there, and when it came to actual fighting, the men could move no faster than in Napoleon s time – if as fast. For on the enemy side of the line, which was slowly moving backwards as the British slowly advanced, the Germans were retreating along their railway systems while the British were leaving theirs behind to advance on foot across a strip of shattered ground. Reinforcements could invariably arrive by rail to a threatened position before the attacking side could break through on foot, and defence on the Western Front always remained mechanised, whichever way the battle swayed, while attack did not.

The shattered battalions were now replaced by others from further north. The Royal Fusiliers, just outside the area of fighting, were told they were to be exchanged with the 5th North Staffords from Gommecourt. "Two officers and thirty-five men appeared," one of their officers said. "The company officer was strung up to breaking point and the junior subaltern could not stop shuddering." The Royal Warwickshires, as they moved up, passed men who had just been withdrawn. The Warwicks' companies, about 200 strong, were as large as the battalions they relieved.

The only chance of a breakthrough was on July 2nd when the rubble of Fricourt was captured without fighting and when Ovillers was entered by men of five different battalions, but the chance was lost through the hesitation of General Horne, of XV Corps, and it never returned again. Opportunity slipped further away when, for July 3rd, Rawlinson merely ordered a renewed attack on the left and centre. The truth about the casualties was seeping through at last and his spirits fell as he saw his worst forebodings about the attack borne out; but so far the picture was still confused and he felt obliged to continue. At G.H.Q., however, the facts were clearer, and Haig, anticipating some success on the right, so reduced Rawlinson's attack to strengthen the south that it achieved little but casualties.

Haig was by now convinced that he should press hard in the area where there had been some progress, but Joffre insisted that, as a preliminary to any major attack on the right, he should capture the Thiepval-Pozieres ridge in front, which could threaten any move forward. The long interval before any advance was made on the German second line was made even longer because Haig was now determined, before attempting his main stroke, to nibble away at the outlying enemy strongholds, which he felt threatened his attacks. Thus, the Germans were given an opportunity to harden and strengthen their hold on the commanding ridge.

The British commanders were racking their brains over the problem of how to capture the German second position, for the Germans were building their rear trenches faster than the front ones could be taken. Rawlinson realised that unorthodox measures were needed. In spite of Haig's objections therefore, he revived the long-neglected idea of surprise and framed a night attack to break the defences on a four-mile front between

Delville Wood and Bazentin-le-Petit after only a five-minute barrage. His boldness was justified. Twenty-two thousand men were assembled after dark within 500 yards of the German line without the Germans suspecting anything, and on July 14th the whole German second line was overrun and the troops passed beyond. On the right, however, Delville Wood was bitterly contested and the South Africans were there called upon to make their supreme sacrifice.

However, on the left, open country lay at last before the assaulting troops, for, soon after midday, the German resistance began to disintegrate. But by the time the cavalry – that cavalry of which so much had been expected by Haig – was able to move forward over the broken, shell-torn, wire-strewn ground, it was too late. Machine guns had been brought up and they had to retire with heavy losses. The battle from this point degenerated into one of attrition.

–

With the Germans now fully aware of Haig's intentions and with the chances of a decisive victory growing more slender every day, Haig resorted again to local attacks in an attempt to enlarge his hold on the rising ground and straighten the British line. The casualties in the second week of the Somme, as much due to the stubborn courage of the Germans as the enduring bravery of the British, averaged about 10,000 a day, though, as the battle progressed, they fell to 2,500, when it was felt that the tide was turning. Haig had modified his early optimism by this time but still had hopes of a break-out.

To capture the ridge, Gough was given the Australian division of Sir William Birdwood, who had commanded them at Gallipoli, and failed so badly with them that the Australian official historian later wrote "the method [of attack] appeared merely to be that of applying a battering ram ten or fifteen times against the same part of the enemy's battlefront." Twenty-three-thousand men were expended to gain a tiny tongue of ground just over a mile deep, honeycombed with smashed trenches and stuffed full of decomposing bodies.

Lieut. J. A. Raws, of Melbourne, wrote home to say that the strain had sent two officers in his unit mad. As he struggled to dig a shelter under the tornado of shells, he was buried twice and thrown down several times, covered with dead and dying. On one occasion, struggling free, he tried to rescue what he thought was a living man next to him and found it was a decayed corpse. "The horror was indescribable," he said.

The ground was "a churned mass of debris and bricks, stones and girders, and bodies pounded to nothing". Of the thick woods, there was nothing left, not a tree trunk, not a leaf or a twig. The wounded who were carried to safety were laughing with relief at the thought of being out of it.

"We are lousy, stinking, ragged, unshaven, sleepless," wrote Raws. "I have one puttee, a dead man's helmet, another dead man's gas protector, a dead man's bayonet. My tunic is rotten with other men's blood, and partly spattered with a comrade's brains." The prevailing tactics were so dreaded and detested that, where it had once been considered a disgrace among the Australians to be sent home, now men were praying for it.

In the last letter before his death, Raws wrote of the "murder" of many of his friends through the "incompetence, callousness and personal vanity of those high in authority".

"For Christ's sake," said another Australian, "write a book on the life of an infantryman, and by so doing you will prevent these shocking tragedies." "We have just come out of a place so terrible," wrote Captain G. L. Maxfield, of Victoria, "that a raving lunatic could never imagine the horrors."

Yet nobody in the rear, neither Haig nor Gough, nor even the Australian commanders themselves, had any idea what it was like.

Following these battles, many Australian soldiers at the front refused to vote in favour of conscription at home. Their one concern was that a sufficient number of men should be left alive after the war to develop their empty country. Here, their commander, Birdwood, lost much of the popularity he had gained with them at Gallipoli, by failing to stand up against Gough's ruthless demands on him for quick results. Haig, always an advocate of the Western Front and always prejudiced against men who had fought at Gallipoli, was unsympathetic and thought the failures were due to the ignorance, conceit and over-confidence that had been engendered by the Australians' success in the East.

These assaults on Pozieres were matched by the shambles on the other flank where division after division tried to reach the petty prize of some obscure village, felt it within their fingers for a moment only to lose their hold again. To the men in the line, it was a period of hopeless confusion, with orders that seemed to them impossible. In spite of pleas from the men in the line that their objective could be approached after dark and rushed at first light with ease, one unit was sent again and again in broad daylight against Mametz Wood, although every attempt was met by frontal and enfilade machine gun fire and shells. Finally, the brigadier in charge stopped it with the comment: "They want butchers, not brigadiers."

By this time, said an officer of the Royal Welch, the wood was only a confused area of destruction with "fallen trees, shell-holes, a hurriedly-dug trench beginning and ending in an uncertain manner, broken branches with their sagging leaves, an unopened box of ammunition, sandbags half-filled with bombs, a derelict machine gun propping up the head of an immobile figure in uniform, with a belt of ammunition drooping from the breech into a pile of red-stained earth." There were wire entanglements and undergrowth, and constant smoke and occasionally flames as the place caught fire.

Continually, the soldier on the move, struggling to advance, kept having to fall flat on his face when "the whistle of an approaching shell grew into a shrieking YOU, aimed at the ear to paralyse before it killed", then rise and stumble on again through a cloud of bitter smoke. Men could not push through the tangle. Years of neglect had turned the wood into a formidable barrier.

Trees and branches formed a barricade, and equipment and corpses were everywhere – more corpses, in fact, than living men. "At the southern end of the wood, the air was sickly with corruption, crushed bark and fresh earth, and the smell of newly cut timber." Shelling had made the scene nightmarish with mutilated bodies and severed limbs hanging among the branches.

Trones Wood in the same area, to Brigadier Frank Maxwell, V.C., who had been an aide-de-camp to Kitchener, was "the most dreadful tangle of trees and undergrowth imaginable, with deep yawning trenches criss-crossing about it, every tree broken off at top or bottom and branches cut away, so that the floor of the wood was almost an impenetrable tangle of timber, trenches, undergrowth, etc., blown to pieces by British and German heavy guns for a week. Never was anything so perfectly dreadful to look at... particularly with its dreadful addition of corpses and wounded men..."

Disregarding the orders of higher authority, Maxwell used his own initiative and pulled a line of disorganised attackers after him, making them advance with fixed bayonets, leaving the wounded behind them in the tangle of branches. Some of these wounded were left for seven days, others remained undiscovered until the war had passed them by and they were beyond help.

But Haig could still record in his dairy: "I had occasion a fortnight ago to call the attention of Army and Corps commanders ... to the lack of smartness, and slackness of one of its Battalions in the matter of saluting when I was motoring through the village where it was billeted..."

He still did not know what it was like up in front. There was still no conception at G.H.Q., and still no one bothered to find out.

Fourteen: The end of idealism

During all this period, as the slaughter went on and the nights drew in and the days became colder, the newspapers at home were hailing the Somme as a major breakthrough.

The first intimation of the attack came within a few hours, with huge posters across the country, GREAT BRITISH OFFENSIVE BEGINS. Snippets of news made great play of the unimportant villages that were captured, but there was little or no mention of the distances covered or the enormous price paid in casualties. In fact, the press knew nothing and, in the absence of hard news, conducted a disgraceful campaign compounded of fiction.

They were not entirely to blame, however. Censorship was rigid and they were fed their information by G.H.Q., and the first official report sent to London made much of the methodical capture of the enemy s first system of defence on a sector of 14,000 yards – but made no reference to the fact that the whole of the rest of the front had come to a stop in appalling bloody disaster.

Not quite everyone was hoodwinked. It was known that the Germans had called off the attacks on Verdun on June 11th and that the French had passed to the offensive, and as early as August 1st, Winston Churchill, at that time an unemployed colonel from France and a politician without a government job, sent a memorandum to F. E. Smith, the Attorney General and a member of the cabinet, in which he asked what on earth our troops were fighting for. They were not making for any point of strategic or political consequence, he pointed out. "The open country towards which we are struggling by inches," he said, "is utterly devoid of military significance. There is no question of breaking the line, or letting loose the cavalry in the open country behind, or of inducing a general withdrawal of the German armies in the west."

The memorandum was circulated, and even read by the King, but to no effect. Haig had his friends, and Lloyd George, who probably agreed with Churchill, was never in a strong enough position to do anything about it. Meanwhile the slaughter continued and the cheerful communiques kept appearing.

The truth, however, was that battalions, brigades, divisions were going forward into the maelstrom and were merely soaking into the ground. Because of the death roll, it was hard to find able men to command, and some extraordinary promotions were taking place. Most of the best were already casualties. More and more men came up, and the artillery never stopped firing, while the skeletons of the dead of July 1st still lay in rows, huddled in the hollows and heaped against the wire. "It seemed to be nobody's job to bury them," and the generals were already busying themselves with new plans.

By this time the young men in the trenches, so full of gaiety, eagerness and faith when they had arrived at the front in May and June, had become far removed from the image of the cheerful Tommy Atkins created by the press, who were said to regard killing Germans rather as a "sport similar to ratting". A few men had deserted and one or two had even been shot for cowardice, but they were not blamed by those who survived for there no longer seemed any sense in the fighting. And they could only laugh aloud at newspaper reports that pretended that July 1st had been a victory. Everyone who had been on the Somme for a week was a cynic.

Plagued by lice, they lived amid all the awful debris of war: dead transport animals, wire, bombs, empty tins, rags, broken rifles, rounds of ammunition, mess-tins, bits of leather and webbing, broken British and German steel helmets, iron stakes and even skulls picked clean by the rats. Here and there were improvised graves, and occasionally an unwary foot treading in the earth of the trench floor would disturb hundreds of white maggots.

They had seen men weeping as they struggled through the grey-white mud that grew worse with every day, and seen corpses used as parapets and even as doorstops. They had seen their friends rotting in the summer sun, "so horrible in their discolour that it called for an act of faith to believe that these were once men, young men sent to this degradation by their fellow men". To these veterans, a break from the trenches was like heaven, and silence away from the racket of war was "a joy, a positive and acute pleasure".

"Would any of us," wrote one of them, "be allowed to live, to love, to marry and beget children, to taste the pleasures of all that a full life promised?"

These men, many of them mere boys still, held the whole world in contempt. One of them wrote: "I think with almost physical sickness of the legends that sustain our armchair patriots at home." Decorations had become meaningless to them, because they knew too many were being handed out behind the line to men who planned the "stunts" that destroyed them – stunts made from maps without regard to actual conditions and without their creators ever experiencing a fraction of what they were enduring. They felt growing sympathy for their German opposite numbers, whom they considered suffered from exactly the same evils as they did themselves. They detested all staff, war correspondents and politicians.

No matter what they read in the press, the battle they knew had been an unredeemed defeat. The enthusiastic volunteers were enthusiastic no longer. They had lost faith in their cause and in their leaders, in everything except loyalty to their comrades. The war had ceased to have a purpose and was now merely a contest of endurance. The Somme set the picture by which future generations remember the First World War – brave helpless soldiers disillusioned by blundering obstinate generals who achieved nothing in return for systematic slaughter.

As August progressed, even the powers at home began to grow restive at the appalling casualties and were wanting to know why the French were more successful with smaller losses. The news, in spite of Charteris at headquarters, was leaking back. Casualty lists were there for all to see and wounded men who had gone home had not kept silent. In some northern villages, bewildered people were wondering how it could have happened that all their young menfolk had been swept away in a single day in a battle that the newspapers were calling "a major victory".

Very soon after the battle started, General Sir Henry Wilson, later to become a Field-Marshal and Chief of the Imperial General Staff, had been hinting that something was wrong with the tactical handling of the troops, and members of the government were regarding the Commander-in-Chief as a "butcher". Even Sir William Robertson, Chief of the Imperial General Staff and always a supporter of

Haig's, confessed himself baffled as to what Haig's objectives were and began making nervous representations to his friend. "The powers that be are getting a little uneasy with regard to the situation," he wrote. "The casualties are mounting up and ministers are wondering whether we are likely to get a proper return for them ... They will persist in asking me whether I think a loss of, say, 300,000 men will lead to really great results because, if not, we ought to be content with something less ... It is thought that the primary objective – the relief of Verdun has to some extent been achieved."

Haig's reaction – "not exactly the letter of a C.I.G.S. He ought to take responsibility also" – was scarcely justified for, though Robertson had always supported Haig, he could hardly be expected to accept responsibility for his plans.

For a while, anxious to keep the government behind him, Haig inaugurated no large-scale attacks, and actually succeeded in making the politicians feel he had been right in his tactics, though Lloyd George at least remained unconvinced.

Visiting the front about this time, Lloyd George was startled to find elation at headquarters. When he ventured to express his doubts about a breakthrough and whether cavalry could ever operate on a front bristling for miles behind the enemy line with barbed wire and machine guns, both Haig and Joffre "fell ecstatically" on him, and Joffre explained that he expected the French cavalry to ride through the broken German lines on his front the following morning.

"The conversation," said Lloyd George, "gave me an idea of the exaltation produced in brave men by a battle. They were quite incapable of looking beyond or around or even through the struggle just in front of them."

"They were waiting," he said later, "hand cupped to ear, for the crack that would signify the final break in the German barrier."

Though he was always in complete agreement with the generals in wanting victory, from this point on he could never agree with the methods they used to achieve it.

Completely distrusting British military leadership, he appointed Sir Eric Geddes, a railwayman, to take charge of transport arrangements in France. He even went so far as to try to pump Foch, the French commander on the spot, for information with which he could condemn Haig. Foch, following the freemasonry of Higher Command, did not let his fellow-general down and hastened to inform Haig of their conversation. Haig, who had never liked Lloyd George, was outraged. From calling him contemptuously "this fellow", he advanced to stronger terms. However, he was well aware of Lloyd George's power and was careful not to pit his strength against him.

As for Lloyd George, he never overcame his detestation of Haig. At his home at Churt, long after the war, he indicated a full-length picture of Haig and, placing his hand across the top of the soldier's gleaming cavalry boots, said "He was brilliant – up to there."

From this period onwards, his hatred of the military oligarchy grew steadily, until he became convinced that the only imaginative general in France was Sir John Monash, an Australian Jew, who was not even a regular soldier. He tried his utmost to remove Haig and his supporters – "we are all asked to bow the knee before this military moloch," he said – but, even when he became Prime Minister in the winter of 1916, he was never powerful enough against the entrenched influence behind the Commander-in-Chief. Even when

Lloyd George removed his ally, General Robertson, from the War Office, Haig still managed to hold on, though his seat remained insecure for the rest of the war.

Fifteen: The tanks

By the end of August, Haig's obsession with the outlying strongholds of the Germans was satisfied, and the British line was straight enough on a seven-mile front for Rawlinson to record in his diary "the Chief is anxious to have a gamble with all the available troops about September 15th". Facing the truth for once, he added: "We shall have no reserves in hand, save tired troops." He might have added also that there was nothing much to gain, for the crisis at Verdun was long since past. But Haig by now was as conveniently committed to the belief in attrition as he had been originally to the hope of a break-out, and in an attempt to prove that the wastage of life had not been in vain, had begun to justify his actions by claiming that attrition had been his policy all along.

Units were rounded up for the new assault, the messages speeding to Happy Valley, the meeting place for divisions moving up to the trenches and for broken units moving back.

"Its brown banks," said an officer who knew it, "seemed to hold a million men and a million animals. All day long the dust, brown and golden in the sunlight, rose and choked the blackening trees. All day long, carts, wagons, men and horses went by. All day long, a Royal Scots band practised *A Broken Doll*."

There was disease in the hot stifling valley. Four out of a draft of five officers went down with dysentery within a few days of joining. Bloated flies hummed determinedly about the cookhouses and men grew sick from the food they contaminated.

In the new attack tanks were to be used. This novel engine of war had been produced against all the opposition of the War Office by a small band of enthusiasts encouraged by the questing mind of Winston Churchill. Although Churchill had been at the Admiralty at the time, he had fostered the idea (with Admiralty funds) when the War Office had failed to show interest.

The first machines sent to France in the middle of August were received with amused tolerance or contemptuous scepticism by most people at G.H.Q. According to Colonel (later Major-General Sir) Ernest Swinton, the man chiefly responsible for raising the new tank corps, "they were looked upon as a kind of toy and called upon to give frequent displays for staff officers." Soon they had become a star variety turn and "were expected to perform twice daily, being asked to knock down trees and other tricks".

Swinton and others protested against these stunts and exhibitions, which were wearing out men and machines, and one officer, Colonel Brougham, a former Staff College graduate, felt so strongly about the displays that Swinton was advised to replace him with another officer. No reason was given beyond that "he was difficult". Eventually, both senior tank officers lost favour with G.H.Q.

Swinton himself was finally removed from command of the new unit and an outsider appointed.

In complete disregard of the pleas of these men and of the French who were in on the secret, and in spite of the fact that they themselves had long before agreed not to use the tanks in small numbers, High Command mustered only forty-nine and once more the cavalry were gathered for the breakthrough.

"I cannot wait any longer for them," Haig wrote of the tanks, "and it would be folly not to use every means at my disposal in what is likely to be our crowning effort of the year."

Lloyd George, told of Haig's decision, informed Churchill and both men explained to the Prime Minister the need to keep the secret of the tanks until there were sufficient of them to have a dramatic effect on any battle in which they were used. They begged him to intervene so that their surprise value was not wasted by lack of preparations, but the vacillating Asquith never had the nerve to stand up to Haig and nothing was done.

In the end, only nine of the few tanks that went into action were able to give any genuine assistance to the infantry and they were so scattered as to have little real effect. Used properly, they might have achieved spectacular results for, according to one German regimental history: "The arrival of the tanks ... had the most shattering effect on the men. They felt quite powerless against these monsters." A British airman at the height of the battle for the village of Flers reported, "A tank is walking up the High Street... with the British Army cheering behind it."

But the secret was out, thrown away, in the words of Churchill, "for the mere petty purpose of taking a few ruined villages". All it achieved was a small gain on the left. However, another big attack on September 25th forced the Germans to evacuate Combles on the right flank. The next day Thiepval fell at last.

These advances were written up as tremendous victories at home. London morning papers went to town, using – although no correspondents had been present – such glowing terms for the tank as "land dreadnought" and "jabberwock with eyes of flame". Many lurid stories were spread; it was said that the tanks carried crews of 400 and were officered by airmen who had lost their nerve. But in fact, the tanks of 1916 could do only five miles an hour and were a sitting target for experienced gunners. They certainly frightened the first enemy troops that they encountered, but the Germans soon recovered and worked out tactics to defeat them. Some of the tanks were successfully stopped by grenades, and the battles of September degenerated into the usual numbing slaughter.

It was at this time, too, that the Royal Flying Corps for the first time began to lose its complete mastery of the air.

The Germans had also reorganised their pursuit squadrons and had received the new Albatros fighter, which fired two guns through the propeller. Oswald Boelcke, one of the first air fighters of the war, came up to the front with a new squadron, which included among its pilots Manfred von Richthofen, destined to become the greatest air ace of them all. But the Allies were not without their own skilful pilots. Albert Ball, V.C. was already in active service, and, towards the end of the offensive, James McCudden, who rose from air mechanic to major with the V.C., was flying on this front, while down in the French sector there was the famous Georges Guynemer.

By now Rawlinson was aware that success had eluded them for that year, but Haig was still calling for pressure "without intermission", He considered the enemy very tired and about to crack, and was being pushed by Joffre who wanted German divisions drawn away from where the French were beginning to regain ground at Verdun. But he was either unable or unwilling to recognise that his own men had reached such a point of strain that, even if the enemy were to collapse, the British forces would be unable to take advantage of it.

"No one who has not visited the front," one corps commander observed pointedly, "can know the state of exhaustion to which the men are reduced."

Meanwhile, the early onset of the autumn rains made the chances of a decision more slender every day. The overworked and badly mended roads finally gave way. The ground became a morass in which men and guns and transport bogged down. Attacks under such conditions were terribly handicapped and failure almost inevitable. Even if a trench were gained, the difficulties of consolidating it liquidated the gain.

Crozier, who had become a brigadier by now, was in a sector where nothing remained of six French villages except rubble and brick mud. The ground was so bad that it was impossible to carry up the timber, wattle and corrugated iron for trenching. "The fields of corn," he wrote, "were now seas of mud." In Rancourt Valley, just off the duckboard track – the long winding route along wooden slats, which was the only safe way to the front through the mud and the shell-holes – he was able to count 102 unburied French dead and SS German machine gunners, still lying by their guns, the cartridge belts and boxes still in position.

The mud clogged on the soles of boots until they had become the size of footballs, making every step an effort. One false move meant drowning, and conditions were "so vile that no man could endure more than forty-eight hours in the forward puddles". No wheeled traffic could approach within three miles of the forward pits. Roads had disappeared and mules and men died nightly in the shell-holes. Rifles became jammed with the mud, and advancing men lost not only boots and socks but sometimes even trousers. To move an eighteen-pounder gun, twelve horses were needed, and corrugated iron sleds were often of more use than wheels. Men were up to their waist in sticky slime and no one could attack through the morass. Both sides were glued to the ground.

Nevertheless, small "stunts" were still called for by headquarters and even attempted, but by October 12th even Haig had accepted that he could never pierce the German defences that year. Joffre and Foch, however, those "twin souls of optimism", continued to urge him on until, at last, Lord Cavan, commanding XIV Corps, which had replaced Congreve's XIII Corps, desired to know whether it was intended "deliberately to sacrifice the British right to help the French left". Other corps commanders had less moral courage and Rawlinson continued to yield his better judgment to Haig's determination. A hopeless series of petty attacks followed, which were obscured at the last minute by a welcome if unexpected last-hour success by Gough along the Ancre.

Sixteen: Empty victory

The Battle of the Somme died, mourned by no one.

The fighting in Gough's final attack lasted for five days, though why it was persisted with even that long is difficult to understand. There was no chance of a breakthrough – even Haig was by now so disillusioned he had at last drawn back most of his cavalry – and as there was no hope of capturing anything worthwhile (because there was nothing there to capture) the British army was like a boxer hitting out at empty air. The special idiocy of this last phase was that, having won, with so much suffering, the high ridge with its commanding observation over the German lines, the advantage was thrown away by fighting beyond it into the depression at the other side. The result was that the British troops were forced to spend the winter in flooded trenches.

It was now bitterly cold, with temperatures mostly below freezing point. A few more ruined villages were taken, but Gough's new Fifth Army suffered the usual heavy casualties. It was here that Field-Marshal Lord Freyberg, then a young colonel, won his V.C. but, in spite of the heroism of individuals and the endurance of the soldiers generally, little was gained. The mud had become impassable round the German trenches where the bombardment had stirred it up into a quagmire. On the night of November 17th, snow fell for the first time and on the 18th the trenches were blotted out by a blizzard. The battle came to an end with a despairing sense of utter futility and waste, and with such a drain on the British forces that the damage to the Germans was completely nullified.

General von Ludendorff, who had taken over command by this time, considered that on the whole the battle had ended favourably for the Germans. There had certainly been no break-out and no town of any size had been taken. Bapaume, one of the objectives for the first day, was not captured until nine months later, in March 1917, when the Germans obliged Haig by shortening their lines and allowed him to walk in unhampered. There was nothing to show for the thousands of lives that had been laid down, only a few miles of blood-soaked ground and a few villages, which had been so pulverised they were no longer of any use to anyone. If this was a victory, it was indeed a strange one.

–

The Somme was Britain's first experience since Waterloo of the real cost of a war conducted against a powerful European nation and the shock was brutal. For sustained horror, nothing, not even in the Second World War, ever equalled it. Never for a moment, night or day, had the artillery ceased to thunder or the machine-gun bullets stopped whistling among the broken trenches and ruined fields and villages, with their scattered graves marked by rusting helmets, wooden crosses or bayoneted rifles.

Yet nothing had ever been too much to ask of the weary men. As Churchill said, "…if two lives or ten lives were required by their commanders to kill one German, no word of complaint ever rose from the fighting troops. No attack, however forlorn, however fatal, found them without ardour." Although something of an exaggeration, in essence it was true enough.

But idealism found its grave in the hills and valleys of Picardy. The troops who followed the soldiers of the Somme into the long arc of wretchedness until 1918 were no longer men in the prime of their lives. Never again was the spirit or the quality so high. After the Somme, the French sneered at the British, and the British at the French, and the Australians and Americans at both. Last sons were called up and the conscripts went forward like driven sheep. They sang still, but never again as they had in the summer of 1916.

Von Falkenhayn claimed that the Somme's influence on the further course of the war was "in no way proportionate to the sacrifices of the Entente..." and Hindenburg, who took his place as Chief of Staff when he was removed from office, said: "If our Western adversaries failed to obtain any decisive results ... it must be ascribed to a certain unimaginativeness in their generalship."

In spite of what they said, however, the Germans had been worse hurt than they suspected. By the end, every available German division had been drawn into the battle. And their losses were all the greater for Von Falkenhayn's order, issued with a lack of imagination that equalled anything from the British High Command, that "not a foot's breadth of ground must be voluntarily abandoned".

It is clear from the records that what the Germans suffered on the Somme surpassed all their previous experience and paralleled anything that happened on the British side of the line. The spirit of heroism that had prompted their stubborn defence was never found again after 1916. As with the British, the men who came later had not the steadfastness and the spirit of their predecessors. The best soldiers, the stoutest-hearted men, were lost. Their numbers were replaceable but their spiritual worth never could be. The Somme was "the muddy grave of the German Army, and of the faith in the infallibility of German leading". The old German army, with its sense of discipline and honour disappeared for ever in the "hell on the Somme".

–

The battle had made hardly any difference to Verdun – or to anywhere else for that matter. It had not, for instance, stopped the Germans transferring troops to the east to crush Rumania when that country had been unwise enough to enter the war on the side of the Allies in September.

The only claim that can be made for the Somme was that, in spite of the appalling losses, the Western Powers for the first time began to feel that they could defeat the Germans in the end. In spite of the shattered battalions, the Germans had not been able to stop their step-by-step advance, painful as it was, and the confidence of the Germans in ultimate victory began to wane accordingly.

But it was a ghastly price that had been paid for the knowledge, and beyond that nothing had been gained by the slaughter. Final victory was probably put further back by the awful losses, and despite the titanic efforts that had been made, the stalemate on the Western Front had remained unbroken. And, as the Liberal leader, Balfour, said, failure to break through looked very much like defeat. All that had been done was to destroy the spirit of Kitchener's magnificent battalions, which, properly trained, fully experienced and supported by tanks in the right numbers, might have performed miracles the following year instead of the British army suffering in 1917 another wretched failure at Passchendaele in Flanders.

In extenuation, it might be said that until the tank there was no answer to the machine gun, and that only human flesh and blood could be pitted against it, and that in 1916 there was no one at the helm, like Churchill in World War Two, with the vision to see what was needed and the authority to insist on it being carried out. (Lloyd George, for all his fire and drive, was always a politician even when he was being a patriot.)

–

Nevertheless, Haig must bear a large share of the blame – even though certain aspects of his plan were forced on him by circumstances. He was no match for the crafty Joffre and, in addition, he was intent on some spectacular achievement. Both he and Robertson had been plagued by what they called "amateur strategists", who produced schemes to divert men and materials from what they considered the main theatre of war in France. They needed a substantial victory to silence these enthusiasts, and Haig was never discouraged by results. Or, if he were, he never showed it. When he changed his tactics to attrition, he was prepared to use his forces to destroy Germans until not a single enemy was left, considering, like Joffre, that he would have won so long as there were still a few Englishmen left on their feet. This kind of crude thinking can never be called strategy and the acceptance of such dreadful punishment for such small results can never be called generalship.

A German writer has said: "Generals operate with human lives ... the total losses incurred in wars conducted by generals can run into millions. A general knows that in wartime he must be prepared to take this hardest of all decisions unflinchingly. That being so, he has no choice but to approach his task with profound humility. He must be fully aware of his special relationship to the highest price a human being can pay – unless, of course, he is inspired by a ruthless quest for power, fatal stupidity or a penchant, conscious or unconscious, for bloodshed, all of which lead, in the last analysis, to murder... How can anyone ever look on human life as a form of war material to be employed with mechanical indifference?"

And surely that criticism, though it was applied to the Second World War and to Germans, must also be applied to Haig.

Yet, unhappily, he was not alone. There were plenty more like him. As Field-Marshal Lord Montgomery has said, the so-called good fighting generals of the First World War appeared to be those who had a complete disregard for human life. Yet they also doubtless felt they were doing their duty – and they did it in the only way they could think of. Clement Attlee considered the fault was that they didn't have to use their brains. "They had too many men," he said.

They applied themselves to the task of breaking the German lines with the intelligence, as one writer has said, of a group of stone age people trying to extract a screw from a piece of wood. Having failed to pull it out by force, it never occurred to them to turn it, and they went on using more and more force, and in doing so they wore themselves out.

However, in spite of everything, it was not Haig and his fellow-generals who were *finally* to blame. The argument that they might have achieved the same end result by standing on the defensive until the tank was ready in large numbers or until the naval blockade defeated the Germans will not hold water. Neither the hard-pressed French nor the unknowing jingoistic British public would ever have allowed it. *Haig had to attack somewhere.* His fault lay in the fact that he could produce no new ideas on how to set about it.

Haig certainly lacked what Lloyd George called "the highest qualities which were essential in a great commander in the greatest war the world has ever seen", but, as Churchill pointed out, "no one else was discerned as his equal or his better." There were no others. The old army, with its emphasis on leave and sport, produced no other kind, and even those generals whose names were not tarnished by the war – those who succeeded in other theatres or in lesser commands – might well have done no better when faced with the problems that faced Haig in France.

They had never been asked to handle such numbers of men before, and they were singularly unfitted for the task. They had never been encouraged to think and, in fact, those few who did were considered untrustworthy eccentrics. Even after the fighting was over and they could look back on their experiences in the cold light of later years, the generals, stiff with the respect for elders and betters they had inherited from Victoria's uninspired armies, still did not have the wits to see what a tremendous engine of war we had produced in the tank. While in England, tradition still clung to horsed cavalry right up to the Second World War, the development of the tank and tank tactics were left to the Germans. The British army under Victoria had produced few men of genius and the British soldier of 1916 suffered dreadfully for it.

The real responsibility for the slaughter, however, must rest finally with the politicians – "the frocks" as they were contemptuously termed by the soldiers – in that they permitted it to happen. At the end of the line, after Haig and the army have taken their share of the blame, it must always be remembered that the politicians had the power to stop it. But they didn't. For all their concern with casualties, they were still playing at politics in London and there was not one of those in power who was prepared to raise his voice or risk his reputation in a firm protest.

Only Churchill objected, but at the time he held no position of authority and was, in fact, in disgrace after the failure of his plans for Gallipoli. Asquith, the Prime Minister – urbane, fair-minded and intelligent – was never the man to run a war cabinet. He was weak and evasive, lacking in ideas, a passive spectator allowing the war to control him instead of his controlling the war. Most of his colleagues were equally mediocre, and infected by place-seeking and self-interest. The result was that, instead of regulating the generals, the war cabinet was regulated, driven, and sometimes even deliberately deceived by them. There was never – not even in the days of greatest crisis – the same single-mindedness or purpose that existed in the Second World War. The concept of total war never emerged in Britain between 1914 and 1918 as it did between 1939 and 1945.

On the one hand, the Somme has been called a useless bloodbath, a bull-headed fight, and on the other the battle that paved the way to final victory. Whatever it was, it was certainly the graveyard of Kitchener's Army.

As late as 1939, and even in 1945, local newspapers in places such as Leeds, Manchester, Newcastle and Sheffield, which raised the battalions that withered away on July 1st, 1916, were still producing whole pages of In Memoriam notices for that day, that day which the generals claimed as a victory. There was never an inquiry into the disaster and nobody ever got the sack.

There have been several battles – Waterloo, for instance, Bunker Hill, and Alamein – which are said to have affected the future of the world. But it can be argued that none affected it more than the Somme – not because of what it achieved, or because it overturned a great power or set up another one, but because of its far-reaching effect on the political history of the next generation.

Six-hundred-thousand allied soldiers were killed or wounded in its unspeakable agony, while the Germans lost another 600,000. A million and a quarter men. A generation of the best of both countries whose deaths led to twenty years of fumbling politics that let Hitler start it all again in 1939. Few of the politicians who took part in the dreary record of the Thirties, ignoring the danger on the Continent and encouraging Hitler with appeasement, had served in France, and those who had were not prepared to risk it all again. The lack of foresight and the despair that existed in the years after the war sprang from the fact that the most intelligent and courageous had vanished on the Somme and mostly only the little men were left.

The nation had been bled white and the memory of the slaughter obsessed the survivors' minds until they could think of only one thing – no more war. Their unrealistic wishful-thinking policies of disarmament and pacifism simply brushed aside what was happening in Germany and left England in 1939 with only a half-equipped army to stand up to the Nazi panzers. Dunkirk and the disasters of 1940 had their origin in the attitude of "it must never happen again".

In their obsession with peace at any price, few European politicians noticed until it was too late that Hitler was not thinking the same way. A show of strength when Hitler marched into the Rhineland or when Mussolini attacked Abyssinia might have destroyed them both. Dictators daren't fail in what they attempt and in those days Hitler was not secure in his seat. Courageous action then might have prevented the Second World War. But there was no strength. It had been allowed to wither in disarmament, in a hopeless search for peace. And there was no courage. It had soaked into the ground on the Somme and in the other slaughters that men called battles between 1914 and 1918.

Who can say how far the troubles of the world today did not stem, via the Second World War, from the Battle of the Somme?

The graveyards on the Somme, some of them seemingly endless, some of them as small and intimate as a cottage garden, lie by the roadside all the way from Gommecourt to Maricourt. The trees have grown again and the villages have been rebuilt and the countryside now, because it's still a backwater and because there are no longer enough survivors to make the 'Tours of the Battlefields' that were organised between 1919 and 1939, looks and lives very much as it did before it was shredded by shellfire in the battles of 1916.

It is still possible to stand on the slopes of the hills and wonder how anyone in their senses could have sent men in rows to attack machine guns across those bare plains. You can follow the routes of the regiments by the names on the gravestones, and on Thiepval Ridge there is a vast memorial, which contains the names cut in stone of the 74,000 dead who have no known resting place.

And as you stand there looking over the countryside in a stillness that is a remarkable feature of the whole area, the feeling of the place is so strong you can almost hear the tramp of feet again or the whine of mouth-organs playing *Tipperary*. The thoughts that come are poignant, a memory of trial, torment and sacrifice.

Nothing can ever touch that frail immortal glory. Even after fifty years, it is impossible not to be stricken silent or moved to the point of tears by the knowledge of what happened on the Somme.

Other books on the Somme

For readers who wish to know more about the Battle of the Somme, there is a whole wealth of literature, written by those who took part, and published between the wars, as well as the war memoirs of the leaders.

Books worth reading include:

Memoirs of an Infantry Officer, Siegfried Sassoon (Faber, 1930).

Goodbye To All That, Robert Graves (Cassell, 1957).

A Subaltern's War, Charles Edmonds (Peter Davies, 1929).

A Brass Hat In No Man's Land, Brig.-Gen. F. P. Crozier (Cape, 1930).

The Passionate Prodigality, Guy Chapman (Nicholson, 1933).

Up to Mametz, Llewellyn Wyn Griffith (Faber, 1931).

At G.H.Q., Brig.-Gen. John Charteris (Cassell, 1931).

Private Papers of Douglas Haig, Ed. R. Blake (Eyre and Spottiswoode, 1952).

Life of Lord Rawlinson of Trent, Maj.-Gen. Sir Frederick Maurice (Cassell, 1928).

Soldiering On, Gen. Sir Hubert Gough (Arthur Barker, 1954).

Official History of the War, Brig.-Gen. Sir James Edmonds (MacMillan, 1932).

War Memoirs, David Lloyd George (Nicholson and Watson, 1934).

Australian Official History of The War of 1914-19, C. E. W. Bean (Sydney: Angus and Robertson, 1935).

The World Crisis, Winston S. Churchill (Butterworth, 1927).

The Battle of the Somme, John Buchan (New York, 1917).

The Real War, B. H. Liddell Hart (Faber, 1930).

Eye-Witness, Sir Ernest D. Swinton (Hodder and Stoughton, 1932).

The First World War, A. J. P. Taylor (Hamish Hamilton, 1963).

The Somme, A. H. Farrar-Hockley (Batsford, 1964).

The Big Push, R. B. Gardiner (Cassell, 1961).

Douglas Haig, John Terraine (Hutchinson, 1963).

In addition, my own *Covenant With Death* presents a fictional picture of the Kitchener Armies and the first day of the Somme.